A Faithful Dad's Guide to Legacy

Travis L. Zimmerman

Editors: Annie Schreiber, Ph.D; Lance Clark
Cover Design by Miriam Eagleson
Produced with the assistance of CreateSpace.

Library of Congress Cataloging In-Publication Data
Zimmerman, Travis L., 1969, Dec. 26
A Faithful Dad's Guide to Legacy / Travis L. Zimmerman

Includes biographical references.
ISBN-13: 9781530470464
ISBN-10: 1530470463

ACKNOWLEDGMENTS

JESUS, I LOVE you with all my heart!

I have loved my bride, Suzanne, from the first seconds I first met her back in 1993 near Wright-Patterson Air Force Base. Soon after we met, this then lowly second lieutenant saluted into her lieutenant colonel father to ask for her hand in marriage. Both he and his beautiful daughter accepted in turn, and I have rejoiced with the bride of my youth ever since.

I love our five children who truly make life worth living: Elizabeth Mae; Koen Irwin; Treyton David; Grantham Everett; and Braden Christian. I thank God for the privilege of being your dad!

A Faithful Dad's board members are delightful servants of the Most High God: Pastor Dave Biser; Yolie DeShong; Dan Gobat; Carl and Nicole Reeder; Cody Wells; and my bride, Suzanne Zimmerman. Your encouragement, guidance, accountability, and love for Christ propel us to joyfully and obediently walk in faith on the path that God has called us.

A very special thank you to my editors, Professor Annie Schreiber and Lance Clark. Your graciousness, tact, and direction were a gift from God Himself – thank you!

*To faithful dads everywhere who desire
to leave a lasting family legacy
by following Christ.*

TABLE OF CONTENTS

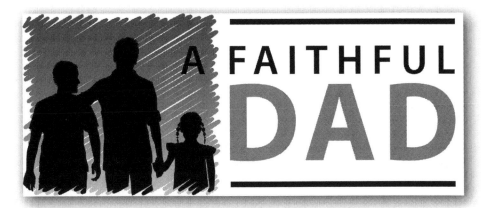

Tag line: Your biggest job. Our greatest passion.

Vision: Follow Jesus. Lead your family. Leave a legacy. (1 Corinthians 11:1)

Mission: Equipping fathers to become faithful dads. (2 Peter 1:3)

Core Values:

- We encourage dads to wholeheartedly follow Jesus. (Matthew 4:19-20)
- We affirm the importance of marriage in transforming families. (Genesis 2:24)
- We believe dads instill their faith into their children. (Deuteronomy 6:4-9)
- We inspire dads to pass along a lasting legacy to their families. (1 Corinthians 3:10-15)
- We motivate dads to build godly friendships in the brotherhood of Christ. (Proverbs 27:17)
- We strive with dads to achieve a healthy life balance. (Ecclesiastes 3:1)
- We desire thankfulness and reconciliation between every man and his dad. (Exodus 20:12)

Introducing A Faithful Dad's Legacy Challenge!

Learning how to be a faithful dad is certainly time well spent, but taking on an accompanying challenge encourages growth. Whether you accomplish this challenge in days, weeks, or months, know that growth comes from consistency and accountability. In other words, join together with a buddy or accountability partner to complete this 12-step challenge (Proverbs 27:17), one challenge per chapter. We'll even ask you to sign it. Some of these 12 challenges will be rather easy for you, and some will be difficult, seemingly impossible. While you're not required to complete every step of the challenge, there is *always* something you can be doing for each challenge step. For example, for Challenge #5, you may already have a good relationship with your dad, so your part in the challenge will be to pray for others. So, here it is...

A Faithful Dad's
Legacy Challenge

Leaving a lasting legacy eternally impacts generations to come.

I COMMIT THIS day to taking on A Faithful Dad's Legacy Challenge:

1. In what ways have you tried to build a legacy that seemed worthwhile, but ultimately could not stand the test of time? Now, ask God to open your eyes to the legacy He desires for you.
2. Honestly answer the big question, "What legacy do I want to leave for my family?" Now, share it with your family.
3. Commit to memory 1 Corinthians 11:1 (NIV), "Follow my example, as I follow the example of Christ." Share it aloud with your family and encourage them to memorize it as well.
4. Praise God, our Faithful Father, for the opportunity to model your own fatherhood after His perfect example. Now, pray this prayer with your family.*
5. If there is a need, pray now that God would soften your heart towards your dad.*
    OR
    If you have/had a good relationship with your dad, simply thank God for this amazing blessing, and then ask God to please heal those families who don't have such a relationship.*
6. If there is a need, forgive your dad, remembering God forgives us.*

OR

If there is/was a spirit of forgiveness between you and your dad simply praise God for this blessing.*

7. <u>If a need exists</u>, reconcile with your father if possible, remembering God has reconciled with His children.

OR

If you and your father have already reconciled or if reconciliation is impossible, ask God to help other fathers and sons reconcile.

8. <u>If possible</u>, contact your dad in whatever method you feel most comfortable with (written letter, phone call, text, meet for breakfast, etc.) and thank him.

OR

If not possible, write a thank you letter to your dad and share it with your family.

9. Consider: What change(s) do you need to make to better live for God? Start today!

10. Consider: What change(s) do you need to make to better live for others, especially your family? Start today!

11. How does Jesus' supreme example of living for God and living for others impact your view of your own lasting legacy?

12. What vulnerable act of service is God calling you to perform? Now, serve outside your comfort zone.

_____   _____

Signature   Date

* Suggested specific prayers can be found at the end of each respective chapter.

FOREWORD

My friend, Travis Zimmerman, is a rare gift to many of us who call him friend. His joy and passion come through so quickly when it comes to His Savior, Jesus Christ, and His love for The Word has made a significant impact on me.

I have known Travis for many years, and his longing to be a great role model for his family has always been first and foremost for him. We both are driven to be the best at what God has called us to be and found worthy of that calling both at home, work, church or community. I feel honored by his request for this forward.

During the past 20+ years I have devoted my life to helping "clean up" the mess of when the family breaks down or falls apart. I have been working with at-risk kids and families in a variety of situations from the streets of New York City as a Family Advocate to surrogate parents at a residential school in Hershey, PA and most recently as the Director of Parenting and Youth at Focus on the Family, creating, executing and facilitating strategy and programs. Through these opportunities I got to know and experience the mess and the wake of hurt left behind by broken families and promises. In my many years of working with these families I could probably count on my own two hands the number of dads involved in their lives. As I engaged these families by earning their trust and respect, I quickly realized that in many ways I was acting as a father to the fatherless.

Raising children is one of the greatest of life's challenges and opportunities but one of the most significant and important things we will do in this lifetime. Dad is the linchpin for their children to know and experience things in ways that no one else can provide in all the glory and messiness of life.

Travis, through his very transparent and authentic way, invites us to go deeper with not only our children but most importantly with our Heavenly Father. He reminds us that the things we long our children to have first and foremost need to come from us. We cannot give to our children what we don't have.

I hope you are encouraged and inspired to do the hard work to be all that your families need you to be and that not only you are blessed by this but your families will be as well.

I bless him for allowing us into his world and for writing his story.

Roy Baldwin
Jaffrey, NH

INTRODUCTION

A LEGACY ENDANGERED

G ONE?

Her eyes snapped open, blinded by the impenetrable darkness that enveloped not just her bedroom but this dreadful phase of her life, a phase wretchedly measured in years. And, there in the dead silence, her probing hands on the vacant mattress confirmed what her heart already knew.

Gone!

Slowly, the blurred ruby numbers crept into focus: 2:29 a.m. She shot out of bed, nearly stumbling over her slippers, as she blindly dashed to reveal the truth the light switch guarded. Yielding to the pressure of her outstretched hand, the overhead light awakened the reality of her husband's present status.

Gone.

The queen-sized comforter and sheets had haphazardly retreated in a mussed up clump at the footboard where their empty bed now thoroughly exposed her ravaging fear: her husband – my dad, Gary "Smoke" Zimmerman – was gone.

Dementia.

You see, her husband was suffering mightily, dying from a rare form of dementia…and he knew it. And Mom was suffering mightily, tortured with her own knowledge: she knew firsthand the bitterness of this ghastly disease sadly explaining, "You often times hear about miracle cures for cancer and other diseases, but dementia has no cure – it's a death sentence."

Retreating from the master bedroom, Mom repeatedly shouted, "Smoke! Smoke!" as she scoured the otherwise silent house. Recognizing Dad's enormously degraded mental state and his alarming suicidal mumblings of late, Mom reasoned that Dad may have escaped to our summer cabin, just four miles to the east. One cursory look into the darkened garage confirmed Mom's unwanted hypothesis: Dad's truck was gone.

Still dressed in her pajamas and bathrobe, Mom shoved on her slippers, hastily making her way to the cabin. Recently, in light of Dad's suicidal state, Mom had privately conceded to my brother, Eric, and me that when she got home from work each day, she wasn't sure what she was going to find: would Dad still be here…or not? Her car rocketed through the blackness, interrupted only by an occasional streetlight and her own, nagging fears: Would Dad be there?

Approaching the cabin, anxiousness welling up inside her, Mom slowed the car to negotiate the sharp, left hand turn leading to the cabin's pea gravel driveway. The stones sharply crackled under her slowing wheels, loudly announcing her arrival. Her spinning steering wheel guided her investigation as her headlights swept across the adjacent trees like a deer spotter's adventure where they eventually settled on an idling 2007 Toyota Tundra – Dad was here.

Yet Mom felt no relief. What would she find this time? How could she explain this to her family? Her friends? Parking her own car behind the Tundra as any good cop might do, Mom cautiously approached the driver's side cab from the rear. Even before she reached the cab, she spotted Dad's bowed head and the top of his torso – he was motionless.

Was Dad dead?

As she strode even with the driver's side window, Mom was relieved to find Dad alive, though visibly distressed, sobbing in a way no closed window could muffle. But, in addition to his suicidal grief, Dad had brought along some things Mom hadn't expected to see: his Bible and a fully-loaded handheld pistol. Dad's Bible was gently worn, the same one he carried to Sunday worship service each week. His pistol, however, was polished and clean, accurate and deadly, having been sighted in each year at a local shooting range. There was little doubt that, if called upon, it could accomplish the gruesome job.

Mom instantly grasped both the impending danger and the opportunity the situation presented as she gently rapped on Dad's closed, driver's side window. Recognizing his bride, Dad groggily rolled down the window, his face downcast. His head swiveled slowly leftward, Mom now catching both his eyes and his fleeting attention.

Mom then did the only thing she knew would reach him: she leveled with him.

"Don't you DO this thing, Smoke! Consider the legacy you're leaving behind for both your boys and your grandchildren," Mom desperately pleaded.

Dad's bloodshot, dementia-diseased eyes stared out blankly at his high school sweetheart as her direct words sluggishly found their target; Mom unconsciously held her breath as she silently waited and prayed.

And, somehow, in a tangible miracle of God, through the haze of my father's dementia, Dad understood. He actually understood! He would not go home to Jesus by his own hand; no, Dad had implicitly conceded to allowing God to control both his arrival and his final departure. He agreed to return home with Mom and eventually surrendered his massive firearms collection to us through help from the Pennsylvania State Police. Then Dad was escorted to a local hospital's psychiatric unit for the first of his two visits. **WARNING**: I'll share with you in Chapter 12 the horrific details of that first psych ward visit, my life's most vulnerable moment.

Through no fault of his own, Dad's legacy was endangered by circumstances beyond his control, and his lasting legacy was clearly in jeopardy. Yet, by God's grace and Mom's honest approach, Dad's legacy outlasted both his memory and his life. Dad's family and friends attested to this in droves at his packed celebration of life service less than two years later.

And that's the point of this guide: How do we leave a legacy that will live on beyond us?

PART 1

LAYING THE FOUNDATION

1

A LASTING LEGACY

*The grass withers and the flowers fade, but the word of our
God stands forever.*

ISAIAH 40:8 (NLT)

*"The greatest legacy one can pass on to one's children and
grandchildren is not money or other material things accumu-
lated in one's life, but rather a legacy of character and faith."*

~ BILLY GRAHAM

WHAT IS A legacy?

Legacy, as defined by Merriam-Webster, is "something transmitted by or
received from an ancestor or predecessor." In common terms, legacy is how
people both in this generation and beyond perceive our memory: helpful or
hurtful, giving or stingy, joyous or grumpy.

More to the point, what is *my* legacy? That really is a deep question, one which I've devoted this guide to exploring. We'll get to that in a moment, but let's consider a few legacy examples from both past and present.

Some legacies are characterized by their names left behind on inanimate objects:

- The city of Washington, D.C. honoring the United States' first President
- The Martin Luther King, Jr. Memorial remembering the fallen US civil rights leader and activist
- Carnegie Hall memorializing the U.S. industrialist Andrew Carnegie

We need only look to history, including ancient Greece, for example, to witness that a legacy can fade: the crumbling Parthenon, Acropolis, and the Valley of the Temples are imposing but sobering reminders of times past.

Other legacies arise due to personal achievement in their respective areas:

- The Fab 4 (The Beatles)
- The Steel Curtain – Pittsburgh Steeler's defense: "Mean" Joe Green, Jack Ham, Jack Lambert, L.C. Greenwood
- Hershey, PA named after chocolatier and philanthropist Milton S. Hershey

Still others are remembered for their reputation:

- King Nebuchadnezzar for his military conquests and his gold statue measuring 90 feet in height
- Alexander the Great for his leadership and military conquests
- Mao Zedong as the principal Chinese Marxist theorist and statesman

Finally, beyond human achievements (both famous and infamous) we are in awe of the natural world:

- The Grand Canyon at 277 miles long, 18 miles wide, and over a mile deep
- Planet Earth, with a circumference of 24,901 miles
- The Milky Way Galaxy, visible by naked eye on clear nights and over 100,000 light years wide

How quickly we're reminded of both our short time on earth and the vast expanse of our universe. Yet it's natural to wonder what our legacy might be, despite being dwarfed by others' achievements and even more so by the natural world itself. These natural, created wonders are, of course, clear reminders of the Creator who made it all. Could this be where lasting legacies truly emanate?

Now let's first consider a legacy closer to home – literally. What about the legacy you leave your family?

As we consider the tradition of many families, it's common to pass along to our families our knowledge, our preferences, and our habits. Dads are famous for sharing information about safety procedures, such as donning proper eye protection when working with power tools, how to handle yourself in public, including giving a firm handshake while establishing good eye contact, and even about the finer points of packing the mini-van trunk with puzzle-piece like perfection. The fact that I'm a Minnesota Vikings fan even though I've never stepped foot in the great state of Minnesota is testimony to my own dad passing along his own preference in football teams. You see, legacy building began early in the Zimmerman household, well demonstrated by our collective passion for the National Football League (NFL).

Back in the 70's I personally favored quarterback Neil Lomax of the then-St. Louis Cardinals. Not sure how, but I think I dug their red uniforms, something very important to keep in mind when choosing your favorite team! Dad, however, was a long-time Minnesota Vikings, fan – the notorious

"Purple People Eaters" and the legendary #10, quarterback Fran Tarkenton. And Dad endorsed a plan that, in retrospect, proved to be a controversial tactic to bring fans (his boys) onto his side.

The plan was simple and it involved a little bribery: every Sunday when the Vikings played my father would give my brother a dime if he rooted for the Vikings. A whole dime! I mean, that was, like, almost two quarters back then. That was money my brother could put towards his NFL Topps football card collection. Meanwhile, I walked away empty-handed!

My loyalty to Neil Lomax and his St. Louis Cardinals was strong, lasting weeks. Weeks! Exactly four, in fact – forever in the world of a kid. So, as the fifth week of the NFL season was being avidly watched in our house, my five year-old brother, flush with cold, hard cash of four fat dimes, I, too, decided it was time to abandon my beloved Cardinals and jump on the Vikings gravy train. As I'm known to frequently repeat, "For the price of $0.40 I was sold out to the Minnesota Vikings." A travesty to this day, a pain of never ending sorrow and discontent: four Super Bowl losses and several conference championship losses. We Vikings fans know pain!

But a funny thing happened later that same season. Despite the steady income stream of dimes, my brother jumped ship from the Minnesota Vikings to cheer for a team called the Pittsburgh Steelers, who went on to win six Super Bowls. You may have heard of them. Dimes or no dimes, witnessing legendary Steelers legendary running back Franco Harris dodge tacklers en route to an end zone celebration was far more payment than any thin dimes could offer. But Dad persisted with the Vikes, effectively forcing himself to spend the end of four Viking Super Bowls out in our barn, too ashamed by our team's miserable results. Yet, we can all probably agree, even between cute stories, that bribery isn't the best example of how to leave a legacy. But I'll admit that years later I purchased four Minnesota Vikings T-Shirts and crosses for my boys....

Like father, like son: Jesus and Vikings!

Aside from the slightly dubious bribery strategy, Dad also left a few quirky legacies. One was his habit of placing a shoe on the kitchen table to remind himself to do something when he woke up the next morning…and I find myself doing similar antics to remind myself of jobs I'm supposed to accomplish the next day. On a more serious note, Dad left an amazing legacy through how he loved, how he lived, and how he saw life. But whether they're grand gestures or goofy reminders, we are indeed cognizant of our own legacies.

In addition to passing along our legacies through personal contact throughout our lives, a part of our legacy can be passed along after our death through our wills. I'm reminded of my half-joking attempts to cut my own son, Grant, out of our will after he transferred his allegiance from the Minnesota Vikings to the New England Patriots – like father like son! Speaking of wills, have you looked at any lately? Wills run the gamut from pretty standard to pretty bizarre.

Here are some pretty standard will requests:

- My estate is to be equally divided between my children.
- Joe gets my guns; Sally gets my china; Bill can have my rare book collection.
- I bequeath $20,000 to my niece as a down payment for her house.

Some pretty bizarre will requests according to Mental Floss are:

- Heinrich Heine, the German poet, left his entire fortune to his wife, but with one catch: she had to remarry "because then there will be at least one man to regret my death."
- Leona Helmsley, the infamous…hotelier, famously left $12 million to her Maltese dog, Trouble, while entirely cutting two of her grand-children out of her will (for "reasons which are known to them"). Her other two grandchildren didn't get off the hook entirely; their inheritances were contingent upon their regularly making visits to their father's grave, where they would have to sign a registration book to prove they had shown up.
- Charles Millar, a Canadian attorney, died a childless bachelor, but he left $568,106 to the mother who gave birth to the most children in Toronto in the 10 years following his 1928 death. This bequest prompted what Canadians called "the Baby Derby" as mothers raced to win the fortune. Finally, in 1938 four winners split the prize after giving birth to nine babies apiece.

So, aside from these laughable, somewhat bizarre, will stipulations, the inheritance of a life lived for God is the aspect of my dad's legacy I most treasure. My dad's faith was a considerable feature of his life. As I'll highlight in Dad's Man Rules #7 (Chapter 5), faith was important to Dad which, by default, made it important to his family. Unlike my faith of many words, Dad's faith was quiet but nonetheless powerfully influential to us. In addition to attending church weekly, our family was guided by biblical principles with our faith lived out through both works and words. As an example, Dad frequently volunteered his considerable maintenance skills to repairing and improving church property, most often in near anonymity – just the way he liked it. And, like father, like sons, my brother and I served for several years as church janitors as Dad taught us how to clean and care for our church which, in turn, helped the church care for God's people. Lastly, and most prominently, Jesus' Passion Week moved Dad deeply, and I grew up with the confidence of Dad's quiet faith in God speaking voluminously into my own life: he both desired and expected me to carry forward the faith into my own family.

So, again, the legacy we're talking about here isn't the kind that's left in a will, whether common or bizarre. And a legacy isn't about making your kids into an exact copy of a younger you, because that isn't fair to them or you.

Rather, a legacy – a lasting legacy – is about you, Dad, wholeheartedly following Jesus and leading your family to do the same.

Take a moment now to re-read that, and let it sink in. *Our* legacy has little to do with who *we* are and much to do with who *Jesus* is: *that's* a *lasting* legacy.

As fine as endowments are, and as inspiring as building campaigns can be, and as humbling as having a city named after you is, none of these legacies is truly lasting. This reality may have many of us rethinking exactly what it is we're leaving behind for our family. It's not our house, it's not our investment portfolio, and it's not our dashingly good looks, because none of these are lasting. No, it's about something – Someone – much bigger than us.

Which is why in the following chapter we unleash this guide's boldest question....

CHALLENGE #1: In what ways have you tried to build a legacy that seemed worthwhile, but ultimately could not stand the test of time? Now, ask God to open your eyes to the legacy He desires for you.

CHAPTER 1 QUESTIONS:

1. What's one tradition your family passed along to you?
2. A legacy – a lasting legacy – is about you, Dad, wholeheartedly following Jesus and leading your family to do the same. Why is this true?
3. Consider **CHALLENGE #1**: In what ways have you tried to build a legacy that seemed worthwhile, but ultimately could not stand the test of time?

2

LEGACY: THE QUESTION V. THE REALITY

So Solomon did what the LORD considered evil. He did not wholeheartedly follow the LORD as his father David had done.

1 KINGS 11:6 (GWT)

"Now Leroy he a gambler, and he like his fancy clothes, and he like to wave his diamond rings under everybody's nose...and he's bad, bad Leroy Brown..."

~ JIM CROCE

A DARK UNEASINESS crossed his face like the shadow of an enormous Midwest raincloud transitioning into a funnel cloud. Back and forth his eyes darted between the oaken door blocking his egress and the barred window that passively mocked his desire to fly: it offered a tantalizing view of freedom just beyond, but maddeningly refused to yield it. Dad was trapped like a rabid bear in a rusty trap.

Recognizing Dad's rapidly descending mood, Granddad and I continued our broken conversation with him, hoping to distract Dad from the hidden demons waging war on his dementia-diseased brain.

Granddad resumed his questions, "So, how's the food here, Smoke? Are they feeding…?"

"AAAAAHHHH!!!!!" Dad bellowed, interrupting his father mid-sentence as gently as a high-speed runaway train derailing at Horseshoe Curve. The stark room cruelly echoed with silent rage as Dad pumped his fists into the air against an invisible assailant.

"AAAAAHHHHHH!!!"

Then, again without warning, Dad abruptly crumpled to his knees, like the downward blazing Hindenburg Zeppelin, grabbing my hand, dragging me down with him in the swirling maelstrom.

And then something unexpected happened: Dad desperately clasped his hands together, plunging his head forward as he shut his eyes as tightly as any five year old playing hide-and-seeking. He was praying…on his knees.

"DEAR, GOD….," Dad thundered as I kneeled with him in makeshift prayer. I anxiously awaited Dad's next words: what would he say to God?

Waiting. Waiting.

A dreadful silence smothered the room like an abandoned airline terminal.

Stealthily peering through the cracked slits of my concealed eyes, I hazily witnessed Dad laboring to collect the unknown thoughts his shriveled cortex refused to yield through his gagged mouth.

"DEAR, GOD!!!..." Dad reiterated, nearly belching the molasses words forward.

Flushed with blood from my own raging heart, my forehead exploded and beads streamed down my drawn face. I was painfully embarrassed for Dad's failing mental capacity.

I finally drew the courage to open my eyes enough to witness Dad grappling – no, gasping – to find *any* words to say. His face was flushed hot with blood, his knuckles locked in a white death grip. The words would just not... form.

Again he did something completely unexpected, startling me from my own deadening sorrow: Dad reached his right hand forward to my right forearm, locking onto it in a suffocating death grip as tight as a field-improvised tourniquet.

"...YOU PRAY!!!" Dad ordered.

Struck and shell-shocked, I promptly obeyed as any solider would under direct orders from his superior. As Dad's proxy, I fervently prayed God would heal Dad, protect Mom, Granddad, us boys, and our family and bring an end to this nightmarish ordeal. Please, Lord, please, heal Dad here on earth or perfectly in heaven. Amen.

Later, as I exited the facility – something Dad himself would never again be able to do – God placed a sobering thought on my heart. I had just witnessed my father in abject vulnerability, having nearly lost everything, falling to his knees, crying out DEAR GOD to the only One who could help him, the only One who could save him.

And then God really dug in: Here was my dad, literally losing his mind, dropping to his knees to pray to the One who could save. If my brain-sick dad could drop to his knees, calling out multiple times for God, but forgetting what he would say each time, then why wasn't I, of sound mind, also voluntarily and frequently dropping to *my* knees to ask God, the only One who can save me, too? That question would haunt me.

But there was no question in Whom Dad relied on: God, and God alone.

No question at all.

Even in the midst of his illness, Dad was leaving a legacy by his reliance on God. Embarrassingly, I find myself questioning my own personal circumstances – questioning God – and not relying on Him in my life's darkest hours. If anything, I get lost in the questions of my own daily life:

- What should I wear this morning?
- How will my proposal be received?
- When is it going to rain again?
- Where did my hairline go?
- Who's going to win the election this year?

These are all familiar questions, but let's clear out all the clutter, all the unnecessary questions, and focus on the one bold, but simple, question this guide aims to address. This is arguably one of the most, if not *the* most, critical question a dad will ever answer:

The Question: What legacy do I want to leave for my family?

Maybe I'm imagining it, but did the room just get a little quieter? Or did my attention just get focused on the implications *behind* leaving a legacy. You see, leaving behind a legacy can, and often does, imply that I'm already gone – dead! Now *that's* a downer! No need to get all morbid about things, but just consider this: each of us has a finite number of days on earth, a limited time to make an impression upon our family, our friends, and our surroundings. Yet, as we think through it, a legacy isn't just something that you produce at the end of your life, something you just whip up quickly in the kitchen like some microwave leftovers for your kids to gobble down after soccer practice.

No, a legacy is, of course, something that is built up – or torn down – over time, a lifetime to be specific. It's something developed day by day, interaction by interaction with those we love, those who love us, those closest to us. So, when I'm gone from this earth, what will I be remembered for, both good...and bad? That leads us to a reality right now that all of us dads must face:

The Reality: Whether you know it or not, you're already leaving a legacy now. But what legacy?

Whoa! That's right, we're already leaving a legacy. This isn't meant to scare you or bully you into being a particular kind of dad, rather it's presented as practical truth. Each and every dad is leaving behind a legacy just as sure as a beach walker casts a shadow on the sand as the brilliant sun sets in the distant ocean horizon. And those shadows we cast can be pretty long...like the shadows we cast in the lives of our own family.

If you're anything like me, you might occasionally think about how you influence your family. OK, not occasionally, but frequently...about the legacy I leave for my children. Ask my kids what they think of me and they may tell you that I love my family, I like to joke around a lot, I love music, I love physical fitness, I love the Minnesota Vikings, and I love Jesus. If pressed, they may also remark that I'm obsessively clean, that I fall asleep on most movies, including my favorites, Star Wars and The Lord of the Rings. They may even tell you that I gorge out on anything chocolate, and that our hefty grocery bills are largely due to the vast amounts of food I consume. Yep, hardly the stuff that we'd naturally think legacy consists of, but surely my kids will remember me for these behaviors and even a few quirks.

Those are among the flattering aspects of my legacy. Then there are the moments I'd rather forget, or, at least, have others forget. I've coached soccer for 11 years, devoted untold hours designing dribbling, passing, and shooting drills, coordinated everything from team rosters to after-game drinks and snacks, coached games and refereed occasional parental spats, yet one of my former players remarked about me to my oldest son, "Hey, isn't Coach Z the guy who's always on his phone?"

Ouch!

That comment stung more than any shutout my teams ever suffered. But as agitated as I was by the player's candid comment, could I really argue with it?

No, not really.

Some of what he remarked was based in truth, and I got the point as quickly as Lionel Messi dribbling around me: GOOOOOOAL! And it's that little truth that can result in a big wakeup call that forces us to pause. It's the same pause I'm going to ask you to take now:

PAUSE: Stop and think a moment right now about the differences you perceive between your *desired* legacy v. your *actual* legacy.

(Take 5 now…)

I'm going to make the daring assumption that, like me, you've got some work to do.

But is it too late to make a change? NO!

Whether you're young or just young at heart, right now is the exact time to reconsider your legacy. Many of us dads may be scratching our heads right now, thinking, I've tried my way of establishing my legacy, and I'm still not content with the result. After all, we've gotten where we are – that is, establishing our current legacy – by doing it our way. In other words, we are where we are because of who we are. And if where we are isn't where we want to be, might we wonder how we got here?

It turns out there's a perfect way we can follow, which we'll highlight in the next chapter…

CHALLENGE #2: Honestly answer the big question, "What legacy do I want to leave for my family?" Now, share your answer with your family.

Chapter 2 Questions:

1. When times turn tough do you find that you drop to your knees and pray?
2. **The Reality:** Whether you know it or not, you're already leaving a legacy now. But what legacy?
3. Consider **CHALLENGE #2:** Honestly answer the big question, "What legacy do I want to leave for my family?" Now, share your answer with your family.

3

FOLLOW MY EXAMPLE, AS I FOLLOW
THE EXAMPLE OF CHRIST

"This is my Son, whom I love; with Him I am well pleased.
Listen to Him!"

MATTHEW 17:5 (NIV)

"You will know as much of God, and only as much of God, as
you are willing to put into practice."

~ ERIC LIDDELL

THIS CHAPTER'S TITLE is actually this guide's key verse 1 Corinthians 11:1 as penned by the Apostle Paul. This verse, among others, is the essence of leaving a lasting legacy.

As a brief overview, God appointed Paul as an apostle to the Gentiles (see Ephesians 3:8-9). In Paul's world you were either a Jew and therefore one of God's chosen people, or a Gentile. Through his various missionary journeys, Paul established over a dozen churches, including Corinth, Philippi, and Ephesus (i.e., modern-day Greece and Turkey). As was custom, Paul routinely wrote letters to both encourage and admonish his followers, and these letters were hand-carried to the church and read amongst the followers of Christ. Paul essentially served as a spiritual mentor to his churches, and he took great care in guiding, praying, and helping provide for his churches. While it's not known if Paul was ever married, he penned his New Testament writings as a single man with a heart for his "children" – the churches he planted and the followers he nurtured and encouraged. Out of this care for his "children," the members of his church plants, he wrote the verse that models the basis of our own lasting legacy:

Key Verse: Follow my example, as I follow the example of Christ. 1 Corinthians 11:1 (NIV)

Thus, Paul is encouraging his followers to follow him – to model his actions and attitudes – because Paul was following the example of Christ. Paul is certainly not holding himself out as the model of perfection – anything but! In fact, Paul humbly notes in 1 Corinthians 15:9 (NIV), "I am the least of the apostles and do not even deserve to be called an apostle, because I persecuted the church of God." No, Paul recognizes Christ as the model of perfection, so in encouraging his followers to follow him, Paul acknowledged his own duty to follow Christ.

It is *this* model that I'm advocating for us dads concerned with leaving a lasting legacy: that our family would follow us as *we* follow the example of Christ. Remember, a legacy – a lasting legacy – is about you, Dad, wholeheartedly following Jesus and leading your family to do the same.

Let's briefly analyze the two parts of 1 Corinthians 11:1:

1. Follow my example…
2. …as I follow the example of Christ.

"Follow my example…"

Paul was born Saul. Defending his Jewish pedigree, Paul declared to the Philippian church (3:5-6 TLB), "I was a real Jew if there ever was one! What's more, I was a member of the Pharisees who demand the strictest obedience to every Jewish law and custom. And sincere? Yes, so much so that I greatly persecuted the Church; and I tried to obey every Jewish rule and regulation right down to the very last point." In other words, before Saul's conversion to Christ, he was a zealous religious teacher who persecuted, imprisoned, and often sent to death followers of "the Way." If you followed Jesus, Saul was targeting you for pain.

Yet this changed dramatically one day as Saul approached Damascus to accomplish his destructive mission. Jesus, in a blinding flash of light, accosted Saul on the road, asking him, "Saul, Saul, why are you persecuting me?" (Acts 9:4 ESV). Saul immediately recognized the error of his ways and promptly converted from *persecuting* Christ to *following* Christ." In fact, Saul, later renamed Paul, writes in Galatians 1:23-24 (BSB), "They only heard the account: 'The man who formerly persecuted us is now preaching the faith he once tried to destroy.' And they glorified God because of me."

And preach he did!

This same Apostle Paul is credited with writing about half of the New Testament through his letters of love, support, encouragement, and rebuke to the many churches he helped establish. Paul also considered his own legacy (Acts 20:24), but mostly in the teaching he left behind not just for the Corinthians, but for us as well. However, Paul's legacy wasn't grounded in his own preaching legacy – Paul personally knew of One exceedingly worthy to follow.

"…as I follow the example of Christ."

Paul knew that following Christ, the perfect example, would be the only way to lead. In this way alone, could Paul lead his churches; he could be their spiritual "father" because he was leading them in Christ's way.

And what of Christ?

Paul's own beautiful words of Colossians 1:15-18 (NLT) celebrate Christ's magnificent glory:

> Christ is the visible image of the invisible God.
>> He existed before anything was created and is supreme over all creation,
> ¹⁶ for through him God created everything
>> in the heavenly realms and on earth.
> He made the things we can see
>> and the things we can't see—
> such as thrones, kingdoms, rulers, and authorities in the unseen world.
>> Everything was created through him and for him.
> ¹⁷ He existed before anything else,
>> and he holds all creation together.
> ¹⁸ Christ is also the head of the church,
>> which is his body.
> He is the beginning,
>> supreme over all who rise from the dead.
>> So he is first in everything.

And one of my favorite theologians, Dr. Henry H. Halley, who essentially memorized the entire King James Version Bible and could recite it, noted of Jesus:

> Jesus the Christ (the Messiah) lived the most memorable, beautiful life ever known. He was born of a virgin and led a sinless life. As a man, Jesus was the kindest, tenderest, gentlest, most patient, most sympathetic man who ever lived. He loved people. He hated to see

people in trouble. He loved to forgive. He loved to help. He did marvelous miracles to feed hungry people. For relief of the suffering He forgot to take food for Himself. Multitudes, weary, pain-ridden, and heartsick, came to Him and found healing and relief...This is the kind of man Jesus was. That is the kind of person God is.

There is no better example, none more glorious to serve than Jesus Christ. And Jesus' perfect service on earth was essentially marked by sacrifice:

- Jesus LIVED sacrificially: He was scoffed at by the ruling class; He was disregarded by His own people; He was mocked at His trial.
- Jesus LOVED sacrificially: He loved the woman at the well, a widely despised Gentile, who desperately needed His grace. Jesus also taught in John 15:13 (ISV), "No one shows greater love than when he lays down his life for his friends.
- Jesus LED sacrificially: He ensured the masses and His disciples were amply fed before Himself.
- Jesus FOLLOWED sacrificially: He obeyed God's will that He be crucified on Calvary's cross.

This same Jesus died on the cross to take away all of our sins: past, present, and future. As the Apostle Peter boldly proclaimed to the Jews in Acts 2:36 (ISV), "Therefore, let all the people of Israel understand beyond a doubt that God made this Jesus, whom you crucified, both Lord and Messiah!" It's this legacy we desire to leave for our families: a legacy that reflects Jesus Christ. And, while there's certainly merit to passing on different aspects of our own lives (football teams, foods, etc.) to our families, the ultimate reason we dads are here is to reflect a legacy of Christ!

There is definitely a balance to strike between modeling our own example and modeling Christ.

So how do I strike the right balance?

Good question.

You see, many of us dads are struggling. Some of us are doing too much, some too little. Those of us doing too much are essentially leading our kids to follow our own, worldly example. For example, some of us dads want our kids to play the same sports we played as kids, to join the same organizations we joined, and to go to the same school we attended. Those of us doing too little, cavalierly relying on God to take care of our kids, rationalize that they are His anyway. "What can I add to what God's doing anyway?" we may casually ask. So here we dads are: some doing too much and some doing too little. That balancing act, though, feels uncomfortable to us.

The best way I can describe the type of frequent discomfort we'll feel in following Christ is by relating it to an embarrassing personal story about a wrecked relationship with an extended family member I'll call "Sam" (not his real name).

After years of discord between us, Sam and I finally reconciled; in fact we're close family friends. But I'm haunted by my years of despicable behavior.

Several years ago I was praying to God about Sam, painfully recalling my actions during the dark days of our relationship. I literally had a conversation in my mind with God, kind of like Abraham talking to God about saving righteous people in Sodom (see Genesis 18:22-33). Here's how this short conversation went:

"God, please bless Sam and his family. Lord, I'm so sorry for fighting with him all these years. I know that doesn't make You proud when I fight with him. After all, I can do that all by myself, without any help from You. But fighting with him is not what You would have me do."

"On the other hand, God, if I ignore Sam, well, You aren't in that either – I can do that all by myself, too, without any assistance from You.

I reviewed my options…

So, Lord, if, on one hand, I can't fight with Sam, and, on the other hand, I can't ignore Sam, then that means I have to be somewhere in the middle, which means praying for him, thinking the best of his intentions, and loving him unconditionally.

Trapped by my own biblical logic, I protested to God…

But being in the middle isn't comfortable for me at all, Lord. It's like I'm a dog lying on my back, completely vulnerable; I'm just not comfortable there!

Nearly instantaneously I sensed the Holy Spirit's response:

That's <u>exactly</u> where I want you, Travis, right in the middle where you're not comfortable. It's in the middle where you're uncomfortable that I can work My perfect power.

Through the Holy Spirit's guidance I understood <u>exactly</u> what God was saying to me about being uncomfortable in service to our King, because the Apostle Paul speaks to it as well. In fact, it's my "life verse":

[7]To keep me from becoming conceited because of these surpassingly great revelations, there was given me a thorn in my flesh, a messenger of Satan, to torment me. [8]Three times I pleaded with the Lord to take it away from me. [9]But he said to me, "My grace is sufficient for you, for my power is made perfect in weakness." 2 Corinthians 12:7-9 (NIV)

It makes so much sense – it's *so* God! He works in our vulnerability and weakness, because we surrender to Him. We are not giving up, but ceding to Him all authority and power, so that His perfect power yields the results God desires for our lives. He's the perfect example!

And, ironically, it's when we're following Him – again, often uncomfortably – that we most tangibly "see" and feel our God standing right there by us. It is in such situations that we perform the most gratifying, satisfying work on the planet: following and serving our King.

To leave a lasting legacy for your family, keep Jesus in the center of your life and let Him work through your discomfort. Our ways, our words, and our world will perish, but Jesus stands forever. We leave a lasting legacy, not when we build upon the crust of the earth, but when we build upon the cross of Christ!

CHALLENGE #3: Commit to memory 1 Corinthians 11:1 (NIV), "Follow my example, as I follow the example of Christ." Share it aloud with your family and encourage them to memorize it as well.

CHAPTER 3 QUESTIONS:

1. What parallels do you see between Paul leading his churches and you leading your family?
2. So how do I strike the right balance between modeling my own example and modeling Christ?
3. Consider **CHALLENGE #3**: How will you and your family commit to memory 1 Corinthians 11:1?

4

A FAITHFUL DAD: WHO IS HE?

"Abba, Father," He said, "all things are possible for You. Take this cup from Me. Yet not what I will, but what You will."

MARK 14:36 (BSB)

"You're a good, good Father, it's who You are...You are perfect in all of Your ways..."

~ HOUSEFIRES

A FAITHFUL DAD: Who is he?

To keep it simple, we'll analyze what it means to be a faithful dad by considering both components: faith and dads.

WHAT IS FAITH?

Let's first consider the faith component. Merriam-Webster defines faith as, "strong belief or trust in someone or something." That's true. God's Word defines faith in Hebrews 11:1 (NIV), "Now faith is being sure of what you hope for and certain of what you do not see." This isn't a misplaced, wishing-on-a-star hope, or a hope that you might get that ten-speed bike you always wanted for Christmas. No, this faith is a bedrock belief that God will do what He's promised to do. Psalm 18:25-26 (GWT) declares God's faithfulness, and throughout history as shown in the lives of Abraham, Noah, David, and many others:

> [25] In dealing with faithful people you are faithful,
> with innocent people you are innocent,
> [26] with pure people you are pure.
> In dealing with devious people you are clever.

So, what's our role in faith? Here are three key roles:

- **Believing in God:** the author of Hebrews 11:6 (NASB) teaches, "And without faith it is impossible to please Him, for he who comes to God must believe that He is and that He is a rewarder of those who seek Him."
- **Relying on the unseen:** Your eyes will trick you, and your doubts will trip you. The Apostle Paul in 2 Corinthians 5:7 (NET Bible) enlightens us, "For we live by faith, not by sight."
- **Trusting God to do the impossible:** Jesus reveals in Matthew 17:20 (GWT), "Because you have so little faith. I can guarantee this truth: If your faith is the size of a mustard seed, you can say to this mountain, 'Move from here to there,' and it will move. Nothing will be impossible for you."

Believing in God, living by faith and not by sight, and trusting God to do the impossible do not come naturally to most of us dads. Yet they are critical if we are to follow Jesus as we lead our families. These three elements transform a willing father into a faithful dad.

WHAT IS A DAD?

In my view, being a dad is God's highest privilege to men. Being a dad encompasses so much of what God has created us to be. In fact, the prerequisite for being a faithful dad is first of all being a man of God.

Becoming a man of God isn't necessarily a rite of passage, though there is certainly a degree of ceremony in it. I clearly remember turning 18 and my dad warning me that now I could both vote and die for my country. Yikes! No, simply turning a year older doesn't make me a man of God. A man of God is someone who follows after God on a day-by-day basis, growing in devotion to Him. It is a sobering title for sure. The prophet Samuel, in speaking of young David, noted that David was a man after God's own heart (1 Samuel 13:14). That's a high and admirable standard. It entails a desire to know about God, so that you can share Him with your family and others as you simultaneously grow in your relationship with Him.

Then there's the distinction between a father and a dad. Many would say father and dad are synonyms, and they would be right in one sense. I think the two connote different relationships between the parent and his children. A father is someone who is first and foremost the male parent of a child. In some circles, "father" is viewed negatively, as a distant third person association of someone who may or may not be in the picture, someone who contributed DNA to his children but little else. On the other hand, in earlier times, calling upon "father" showed a child's respect for him, even if the emotional distance was blatantly apparent.

A dad connotes a different relationship. When we call our parent, "Dad", there is a warmth, a sense of love, an almost higher calling. "Dad" suggests the relationship between parent and child has grown in intimacy. My own father was a man of steel, tough on the exterior and respected by nearly everyone, but when he got home he was "Dad" to my brother and me. And as tough as Dad was to everyone else outside of our family, he showed his softer side when his grandkids doubled down on this term of endearment, calling him "Dad-Dad." No, in becoming a dad there's isn't an unwritten requirement to get gushy and love-dovey, but there's certainly a recognition of the tender quality of being a dad.

So struck was I by my own dad's love and tenderness that at age five I came to a realization, which I proudly announced to him: "I want to be a dad when I grow up!" Yes, before I aspired to be an astronaut, before I desired to be U2's other lead singer, or before I longed to serve as a United States Air Force fighter pilot, I first dreamt of being a dad. In retrospect, it's really *all* I ever aspired to be. It's not that I didn't have educational nor occupational aspirations (I certainly did), it's just that being a dad seemed grown-up, so critical, so valuable. Little then did I know then how on-target that little five-year-old boy was, and I thank God for placing that desire in my heart when I was so young.

But apparently there's a downside to being a dad, too. In recounting to my kids this story of my lifelong dream of being dad, my then-eight-year-old son Grant dryly quipped, "You know, Dad, being a dad doesn't pay so well." Ha! In truth, I was muddling through my second unemployment, so money must have been on my lips if it had been on Grant's mind. But, while being a dad indeed may not pay well monetarily, there are certainly uncountable joys on earth and treasures in heaven for us dads who savor fatherhood!

Now that we've explored both the definitions of faith and being a dad, let's bring the two together and consider what it means to be a faithful dad.

SO WHO IS A FAITHFUL DAD?

At this point, you may be asking yourself a few of these questions:

- "I've messed up parenting so much already…is there any way I can recover?"
- "Would my family ever consider me faithful?"
- "How could I ever be a faithful dad?"
- "Am I worthy of leaving a lasting legacy?"

These are all tough questions, likely causing most of us to pause. What if I don't like the answers? Am I setting myself up for failure?

As one pragmatic dad who previewed the concept phase of this guide profoundly challenged me, "You need to stress a dad's need to lead this charge and not dump it onto mom. I am a perfect example of NOT leading the charge." That's a humble admission from a dad just like you and me.

From my own viewpoint, I sometimes feel like I'll never be as good as my kids' mom. This isn't a contest, but I want to feel relevant in my efforts to parent our kids. Kids will naturally gravitate towards their mom, but there's a place for dad, too, right? You bet.

Of course, that makes us feel all the more uneasy in our efforts to claim the title "faithful dad." With all the mistakes I've made, the temper tantrums I've thrown, and the barbed insults I wish I would've never said, I sometimes feel like anything *but* a faithful dad. Claiming to be a faithful dad is similar to the feeling I get when I read Jesus' Sermon on the Mount, my favorite of Jesus' messages, as recorded in Matthew 5:3-12 (NIV):

Jesus said:
3 "Blessed are the poor in spirit,
    for theirs is the kingdom of heaven.
4 Blessed are those who mourn,

for they will be comforted.

[5] Blessed are the meek,
   for they will inherit the earth.
[6] Blessed are those who hunger and thirst for righteousness,
   for they will be filled.
[7] Blessed are the merciful,
   for they will be shown mercy.
[8] Blessed are the pure in heart,
   for they will see God.
[9] Blessed are the peacemakers,
   for they will be called children of God.
[10] Blessed are those who are persecuted because of righteousness,
   for theirs is the kingdom of heaven.
[11] "Blessed are you when people insult you, persecute you and falsely
   say all kinds of evil against you because of me. [12] Rejoice and be
   glad, because great is your reward in heaven, for in the same way
   they persecuted the prophets who were before you."

As I read Jesus' words here, I'm absolutely inspired…yet absolutely dejected.
Let me explain. From a phrasing standpoint alone, the poetry of Jesus' words
are gorgeous, so skillfully crafted by the master orator – it's difficult to not be
inspired by Him. Yet, the further I read into the Beatitudes, the more quickly
I become aware of two unpleasant realities:

* First, in the Beatitudes, the qualities associated with being blessed by God
  don't initially sound so blessed: those who are poor in spirit; those who
  mourn; those who are persecuted. I just cannot imagine myself wearing a
  custom T-shirt sporting the phrase, "I'm persecuted … and I'm blessed!"
  People would wonder more about me than they already do!
* Second, as Jesus systematically and poetically articulates the attri-
  butes of those blessed by God, a realization begins to creep over me.
  If I keep reading, or pause on one attribute too long, I may begin
  to sweat. Slowly, I'm able to put into word the thoughts that are

troubling my heart as I read: There's no WAY I could ever do or feel these things all by myself.

And at that moment, it's as if the Holy Spirt snaps His fingers in a loud >>CLICK<<, **"That's EXACTLY the point!** *You* **CAN'T do this by all by yourself: you need Me!"**

Truth! I <u>can't</u> expect to be a Christ follower all by myself – I need the Holy Spirit to go before me, guide me, and correct me.

And, THAT, my brothers, is the point I'm making about being a faithful dad – we CAN'T do it by ourselves. God never intended us to be a faithful dad by flying solo. After all, who by himself could *ever* live up to that standard, that model, that name? None other than God Himself!

GOD: *THE* FAITHFUL DAD!

Armed with this life-changing insight, we begin to see how we can pattern our own parenting after Father God Himself, the perfect model of *the* Faithful Dad. And God's Word is filled with descriptions of His faithfulness.

In Exodus 34:6 (NET Bible), God prepares to present Moses with the second set of stone tablets, after Moses destroys the first in his anger over the Israelites forgetting God. The LORD comes down in a cloud, proclaiming, "The LORD, the LORD, the compassionate and gracious God, slow to anger, and **abounding in loyal love and faithfulness...**" His faithfulness again is demonstrated by being a God of second (and third and fourth...) chances.

In a Scripture passage loved by millions, the prophet Jeremiah sings of God's steadfast faithfulness in Lamentations 3:22-23 (NIV), "Because of the LORD's great love we are not consumed, for his compassions never fail. They are new every morning; **great is your faithfulness.**" That is divine inspiration for dads to rise to each morning ready to receive mercy and grace, no matter what happened in the past.

God is even faithful through our temptation, as we essentially make daily decisions either to choose His way or Satan's way. The Apostle Paul notes in 1 Corinthians 10:13 (NIV) how our faithful God promises to provide an "escape" hatch, a route of egress, in times of temptation: "No temptation has seized you except what is common to man. **And God is faithful**; he will not let you be tempted beyond what you can bear. But when you are tempted, he will also provide a way out so that you can endure it." God not only recognizes our temptations, but he faithfully provides a way out of them when we seek Him!

Yet, God knows we dads stumble, we worry, and we self-doubt. And, yes, if we're totally honest with ourselves, we may even doubt God Himself. In a letter to his protégée, Timothy, the Apostle Paul reminds us in 2 Timothy 2:13 (ESV) of God's unchanging ways, "...if we are faithless, **he remains faithful** — for he cannot deny himself." That's an encouragement we can hold onto when times turn tough.

These are but a few of the dozens of promises of God's faithfulness.

We know that God is faithful. But what of His role as a Father?

Bible scholars have discovered over 700 names for God in the Bible. As we consider the names of God, we remember we serve a Triune God: God the Father, God the Son, and God the Holy Spirit. Each is divinely united as One God in three distinct Persons of the Trinity. God, as Father, is among the most popular of His names. In modeling the Lord's Prayer, Jesus begins, "Our Father in heaven..." (Matthew 6:11). God is referred to as "our Father" 13 times in the Old Testament. Jesus Himself refers to God as His Father over 150 times, and He speaks of God being our Father 30 times.

Most significantly for this guide's focus is one of the intimate roles of God as our Father. While all the names of God are important in their various ways, the name "Abba Father" is one of the most critical for understanding how He relates to people. The word *Abba* is an Aramaic word that would most closely be translated as "Daddy." It was a common term that young children frequently used to address their fathers. It signifies the close, intimate relationship of a father to his child, as well as the childlike trust that a young child puts in his "daddy." Jesus Himself appeals to His "daddy" in Mark 14:36 (BSB) as He agonizes in the Garden of Gethsemane crying, "Abba, Father," He said, "all things are possible for You. Take this cup from Me. Yet not what I will, but what You will."

Throughout the Bible, God's parental care for His children is clearly evident:

- He will cover you with his feathers, and under his wings you will find refuge; his faithfulness will be your shield and rampart. Psalm 91:4 (NIV)
- Father of the fatherless and protector of widows is God in his holy habitation. Psalm 68:5 (ESV)
- One God and Father of all who is over all, and through all, and in all. Ephesians 4:6 (NASB)

So, the basic connection is simply this: a faithful dad endeavors to model God, our Faithful Father. For example, as we'll cover in succeeding chapters, we can model His forgiveness by forgiving those who've wronged us, because Jesus forgave. We can model His reconciliation, seeking peace in our personal relationships, because Jesus reconciled with us. And we can model His thankfulness by thanking others, because Jesus thanks His own Father.

Will we dads ever get there by ourselves? Never. But can we dads make it a goal to please our own heavenly Father? Yes! And we can trust the Holy Spirit to fill in our shortcomings, to do for us what we could never do for ourselves: become a faithful dad to the family God has gifted us with to love, teach, and lead towards Christ. Again, as the Apostle Paul instructs, follow my example, as I follow the example of Christ.

Accordingly, here are some of the values we see us faithful dads holding:

- We encourage dads to wholeheartedly follow Jesus. (Matthew 4:19)
- We affirm the importance of marriage in transforming families. (Genesis 2:24)
- We believe dads instill their faith into their children. (Deuteronomy 6:4-9)
- We inspire dads to pass along a lasting legacy to their families. (1 Corinthians 3:10-15)
- We motivate dads to build godly friendships in the brotherhood of Christ. (Proverbs 27:17)
- We strive with dads to achieve a healthy life balance. (Ecclesiastes 3:1)
- We desire thankfulness and reconciliation between every man and his dad. (Exodus 20:12)

Now *that's* a faithful dad!

CHALLENGE #4: Praise God, our Faithful Father, for the opportunity to model your own fatherhood after His perfect example. Now, pray this prayer with your family:

Dear God, I praise you as our good and gracious Father, and that You want the best for us. Please forgive me for the times I've tried to make my legacy about me when, really, it should be about You. Thank You for setting the perfect example for fatherhood. Please help me to model my words, my actions, and my life after You as I lead my family. Amen.

CHAPTER 4 QUESTIONS:

1. Travis claims that being a dad is God's highest privilege to men, because being a dad encompasses so much of what God has created us to be. How so?
2. How can we claim to be a faithful dad?

3. Consider **CHALLENGE #4**: How will you and your family praise
    God, our Faithful Father, for the opportunity to model your own
    fatherhood after His perfect example?

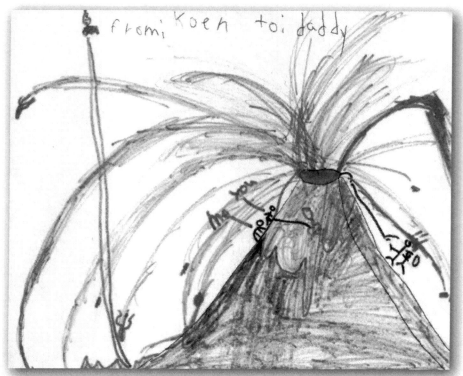

**Our kids will follow us dads anywhere, even up the face of an active volcano!
Note: Koen, our artistic son, drew himself (noted as "me") following "daddy"
(noted as "you") on the left side of this volcano…probably Mt. Doom!**

PART 2

LEGACY: THE PAST IS PROLOGUE

5

But you don't know my dad...

Let us then approach the throne of grace with confidence, so that
we may receive mercy and find grace to help us in our time of need.

Hebrews 4:16 (BSB)

"He broke promises, was abusive physically and mentally, never
was around and caused my life to be a living hell."

~ Anonymous

By God's grace, I was raised by a faithful dad. My dad, though, didn't enjoy the same blessing. To hear Dad tell it, he grew up a lonely, only child because his parents, though lavishing him with gifts, refused to lavish their time and attention he so desperately craved. Sure, there were plenty of forlorn family pictures of the three of them, with fake plastic smiles, all dressed in the latest fashions; but his parents were largely Absent Without Leave (AWOL) and uninterested in his life, uninterested in him. His mother worked every day at her in-home beauty salon from early in the morning until the early evening hours, only emerging between appointments to hastily warm up a meal for him before hurriedly darting back to take care of other clients. His father, Dad was to later learn, intentionally worked second shift at the RCA factory so that he wouldn't have to deal with raising his son. And as involved in extracurricular activities as my dad was, neither of his own parents ever attended any of his school soccer games or band concerts. The reality nearly ate him alive: Dad was deeply hurt and alone most of his childhood. Yet, it was in these years that Dad vowed he would not only capture the good things that his parents taught him, but also, more soberly, that he would alter the broken legacy his own family had left him by turning it for good in raising his own sons, Eric and me. That broken legacy Dad found best captured in the now classic Harry Chapin ballad, *The Cat's in the Cradle*; it moved my dad deeply every time he heard it, a sorrowful reminder of his own father's shattered legacy to him.

I've long since retired, my son's moved away
I called him up just the other day
I said, "I'd like to see you if you don't mind"
He said, "I'd love to, Dad, if I can find the time.
You see my new job's a hassle and kids have the flu
But it's sure nice talking to you, Dad.
It's been sure nice talking to you."

And as I hung up the phone it occurred to me
He'd grown up just like me.
My boy was just like me.

And the cat's in the cradle and the silver spoon
Little boy blue and the man in the moon
When you comin' home, son
I don't know when, but we'll get together then, Dad.
We're gonna have a good time then.

Cat's in the Cradle, Harry Chapin

From this heartbreaking parallel account of my dad's childhood springs a real promise of hope: a faithful dad who persevered to leave a lasting legacy for his family by following our Faithful Father. It's about guys like you and me who also want to be faithful dads, too. And it's not too late!

Fittingly, my dad was one-of-a-kind, "a force of nature" as he was posthumously described by one of my childhood buddies. Dad, a man of few words, nonetheless developed several "Man Rules" that my brother and I learned early on and were a gateway to manhood. Here are some of Dad's "Man Rules" presented here in print for the first time.

AN ABBREVIATED LISTING OF SMOKE ZIMMERMAN'S "MAN RULES"

1. **Spit six feet** – It drove my dad crazy when we would spit, and it would dribble down our chins. "To be a man, you boys need to learn how to spit six feet," he bellowed and then proceeded to demonstrate by hawking up an oyster, propelling it yards away. Shock and awe! It took a lot of practice, but there's not a time that I don't think of this rule when the necessity to spit arises.
2. **A man's word is his bond** – If you say you're going to do something, follow through and do it.
3. **Chivalry is not dead** – Dad always taught us to open doors for Mom, to let her choose first, to defer to her. We were never in as much trouble as when we disrespected Mom. Dad taught us to value our mom, and our future brides, above all else on earth. This next "Man Rule" nails it.
4. **An appreciation for true beauty** – Like many families, our family had "assigned" dinner table seating, kind of like "assigned" church seating. On certain nights, Dad would turn his head towards Mom, smile, then turn to us boys and prompt, "Boys, doesn't your mother look beautiful this evening?" At first, Eric and I were too young to appreciate Mom's true beauty, both inside and out, so our faces would turn beet-red as we buried our forks into our mashed potatoes, much to Dad's dismay.

Each time, though, we were prodded to mutter the words, "Yes, you look beautiful, Mom." Mom blushed, frowning softly; Dad was embarrassed. Nice. Yet, as the years passed and Eric and I slowly matured, Dad continued to repeat the same question, at which point Eric and I competed to be the first to wholeheartedly respond, "Yeah, Mom, you DO look beautiful tonight!" Mom blushed, smiling softly; Dad was pleased. I always thought how sweet that was of Dad to appreciate Mom like that. Decades later, with Dad and Mom both now gone home to be with the Lord, I often find myself asking my own four boys Dad's same tender question, "Boys, doesn't your mother look beautiful this evening?" It came as little surprise that their little boy faces turned beet-red as they buried their forks into their mashed potatoes!

5. **"I'm your father, not your friend"** – Dad noted that we had plenty of friends but only one father. And, as our father, he didn't approach his young children from a peer-to-peer relationship, but as a mentor-to-protégée relationship.

6. **Be there** – Because my dad's parents never attended even one of his extracurricular high school activities, Dad made it a point to be at every one of Eric's and my scouting, soccer, choral, and band events. He never missed a one, even due to illness! Sadly, I cannot make this same claim with our five kids, but I certainly try to model his example.

7. **Faith is important** – We rarely missed Sunday morning church, and there were at least two reasons for this: faith was important to Dad and Mom, and the Methodist church we attended was literally 1/8 mile up the hill from our house. As I quipped at my father's celebration service, we were Methodists not so much by theology but by proximity! Nonetheless, Dad's setting church attendance as a priority stuck with me.

In addition to being given these "Man Rules", we were disciplined frequently and fairly and loved intensely. I can say that, even at a young age, I definitely began to understand a key biblical concept: Dad both commanded and gave respect, and in that, I saw a reflection of what it means to fear God.

I led Dad's celebration of life service in 2011, witnessing hundreds of attendees and dozens of friends and co-workers expressing their respect for my dad through personal testimonies about his professionalism, his policy, his faith, and, most of all, his love for his family. As I watched this, God helped me realize a key pillar of my life: **more than anything else, I, like my dad, want to be remembered most of all as a faithful dad.** It brought tears to my eyes then, and it brings tears to my eyes now even as I type this.

Follow my example, as I follow the example of Christ. 1 Corinthians 11:1 (NIV)

BUT YOU DON'T KNOW MY DAD...

Yes, that's absolutely true, I don't. Some of us have fathers who have already perished. Some of us have fathers we no longer talk to, or who abused us, or who took advantage of us. What I do know, from talking with thousands of men, is that many of us don't or didn't have a faithful dad. One dad cautioned in his review of this guide's initial concept, "Many men are not the product of a faithful father. Nevertheless, a faithful dad seeks to honor God through acknowledging and appreciating his earthly father." I think this dad speaks for legions of us dads, and I pray I've properly and sensitively addressed his concern. This, of course, leads many of us to the same question I often hear, "How can I be a faithful dad when my own dad was such a poor example of a faithful dad?"

You see, unlike for divorce, there is no biblical "out clause" for the father-child relationship. Our culture is filled with stories of dads who let their children down. And this behavior isn't just a recent behavior – it's been happening for a long time.

Charles Francis Adams, grandson of John Adams, our second U.S. President, and son of John Quincy Adams, our sixth U.S. President, served as a Massachusetts state senator, a U.S. congressman and ambassador to Great Britain under Abraham Lincoln. Charles Francis Adams was also very conscientious about keeping a daily journal and encouraged his children to do the same.

Henry Brooks, the fourth of Charles Francis Adams' seven children, followed his father's advice and began journaling at a young age. One particular entry written when Brooks was eight offers an insight of varied perspective. Following a day spent with his father, Henry Brooks penned:

Went fishing with my father today, the most glorious day of my life.

The day was so glorious, in fact, that Brooks continued to talk and write about that particular day for the next thirty years. It was then that Brooks thought to compare journal entries with his father.

For that day's entry, Charles had written:

Went fishing with my son, a day wasted.

Sadly, this is the type of dad many of us are all too familiar with.

Pop songs also painfully relate the real pain that exists when a father doesn't live up to his part:

- U2's Bono, from *Sometimes You Can't Make It On Your Own*, "We fight all the time, you and I...that's alright. We're the same soul. I don't need...I don't need to hear you say that if we weren't so alike you'd like me a whole lot more."
- Everclear's Art Alexakis, from *Father of Mine*, "Father of mine, tell me how do you sleep? With the children you abandoned, and the wife I saw you beat. I will never be safe, I will never be sane, I will always

be weird inside, I will always be lame. Now I'm a grown man with a child of my own, and I swear, I'll never let her know all the pain I have known. Daddy gave me a name…then he walked away.

- Casting Crown's Mark Hall from *American Dream*, "His American Dream is beginning to seem more and more like a nightmare with every passing day. Daddy, can you come to my game? Oh, Baby, please don't work late. Another wasted weekend and they are slipping away. 'Cause he works all day and lies awake at night. He tells them things will get better. Just take a little more time…"

- And who doesn't chuckle along with Johnny Cash's classic tune, *A Boy Named Sue*, "My daddy left home when I was three. And didn't leave much to Ma and me, just this old guitar and an empty bottle of booze. Now, I don't blame him 'cause he run and hid. But the meanest thing he ever did was before he left, he went and named me 'Sue.'"

And these dad heartbreaks don't just occur on the national level – they are local, yet most we don't know about. In my years of interacting with men, many have shared the pain of what it means to have a deadbeat dad:

- "I never knew who my dad was," lamented one man.
- Recalls another man, all too easily, "Dad was so social, engaging, and the 'life of the party' with guests who visited us: some said 'butter would melt in his mouth.' But it was a different story when dad was alone with me. It was all just a big show: he wanted nothing to do with me."
- "My father has passed away already; he was never really involved in my family," grieved another.

Others of us struggle because our dads weren't anything like the faithful dad we wanted them to be:

- "My dad was a monster," bemoaned one abandoned son. "One night he got drunk and came after me with a chainsaw. He's gone now, so I'll never have to see him again."

- Another man revealed, through much heartache, "My biological dad doesn't even acknowledge that I exist. Every year I'll call him on the phone to see how he's doing, and my dad will say to me, 'Why are you calling me? I'm not related to you, I don't care to know you; I don't even know who you are.'"
- Another man struggles because his dad admirably took care of his ailing bride over the course of 20+ years only to crack under pressure and bolt from his family into an adulterous affair, leaving his estranged bride, who died single soon after.
- Yet another man worked all of his life to build a prominent ministry but fell into sin late in his life, embarrassing himself and his family. He was stripped of his ministry leadership.

These real stories are not shared in judgment but in the reality of what has happened, does, and can happen to far too many of us. It would be madness to pass along to our family these examples ranging from passive to destructive.

Regardless of whether your dad was voted "Father of the Year" or "World's Worst Dad", we know that ALL of our dads made mistakes (some more than others), just as all of us make mistakes (some more than others). That's where God's grace enters in. There are many definitions and Bible verses concerning grace, but perhaps it's easiest to remember grace as kindness repaid for a despicable act (sin).

Men have cried aloud to me – not weak men, but tough men from regions as disparate as the coal country of Western Pennsylvania to the snowy New England countryside to the blazing-hot Deep South. We know that the wounds from our fathers run deep, far deeper than we could have ever imagined as a child. Yet, as we pray and mourn together, the Holy Spirit is always quick to remind us that we have a heavenly Father who NEVER makes mistakes, who ALWAYS loves us, who NEVER leaves us or forsakes us. We have a heavenly Father who gives perfect grace for our shortcomings, even sending his Son, Jesus Christ, to die on Calvary's cross in a perfect demonstration of our Father's perfect grace for us. The writer of Hebrews reminds us in 4:16 (BSB), "Let us then approach the throne of grace with confidence, so that we may receive mercy and find grace to help us in our time of need."

Let me preview the next three chapters. If we're establishing a legacy – and we understand we're already leaving one – we also recognize that the past is prologue. In other words, the past can actually be a preview of what's to come as we daily build our own legacy. So, we're essentially looking at all three phases: past, present, and future:

- We have a legacy – for better or worse – that was passed on to us by our own dad.
- We're currently building the legacy our family is receiving now.
- We're, of course, rightly concerned about the future legacy we'll leave our family after we leave this earth.

We can better grasp this three-phased approach if we remember the truth of Hebrews 13:8 (ESV), "Jesus Christ is the same yesterday, today, and forever." Jesus doesn't change – ever. That's an awesome thing, to be sure. He'll help us remember and come to terms with the past, live in the moment, and anticipate the future, just by following Him. This is why it's so vital to follow Jesus' example of a legacy: He did right – then, now, and forever. That's how we leave a legacy that our family will always be proud of, a legacy that will always be remembered. As they say, those who don't remember the past are condemned to repeat it. Now, I don't want to give the impression that we have to do right to leave a legacy. Leaving a legacy has less to do with doing things right, and more with doing the right things. That is, following Jesus and leading your family.

With the passing of my own dad, I've personally experienced the pain, hurt, and unsettled feeling the loss of a father leaves in its wake. That's why I'm turning to Jesus to model the pattern of my fathering and, in turn, the pattern of my legacy. My legacy represents His legacy. It's a good opportunity to recall our memory verse from last chapter: "Follow my example, as I follow the example of Christ." 1 Corinthians 11:1. In that theme are the three steps which we'll be covering in the next three chapters. WARNING: These steps are not for the faint of heart, nor the hardened of heart. They are:

- Forgive your dad (because Jesus forgives).
- Have peace by reconciling (because Jesus reconciled with us). Remember that forgiveness and reconciliation are NOT the same thing: forgiveness alleviates past sin; reconciliation promotes peaceful relations.
- Thank your dad (because Jesus encourages thankfulness).

I can almost hear the sighs, the groans. This is definitely the "heavy lifting" of working and improving our personal relationships: forgiving, reconciling and thanking, when we'd like nothing better than to either actively fight with our father or else passively ignore him like many of us have done for years, even decades.

Regardless of how our fathers treated us, or how we treated them, or what has taken place between us and our fathers, it's critical that we each forgive our father in our heart, just as Jesus teaches us. Remember, unforgiveness is a poison to our soul. Our bitterness may not kill us, but it kills the reconciliation God has for us through true forgiveness of past wrongs. So, if you're just not ready or able to make amends with your father, remember that you have a heavenly Father who loves you dearly. You have a Father who loves you perfectly and will never leave you nor forsake you (Joshua 1:5). Our heavenly Father's example will help us reconcile with our earthly fathers.

Remember, God works through our vulnerabilities (i.e., like a dog on his back) – His power is perfect in our weakness (2 Corinthians 12:9). Whether or not I had a faithful dad...or not, my goal is to follow Christ. We can take some examples from our own dads: things we'd like to replicate, things we'd like to change, and grace always.

That's why I'm issuing this chapter's challenge, and it is no small act.

CHALLENGE #5: <u>If there is a need</u>, pray now that God would soften your heart towards your dad.

> Dear God: I pray that you would soften my heart towards my dad. Regardless of our past relationship, I desire to have an attitude towards Him that would be honoring to both You and him. Amen.

OR

<u>If you have/had a good relationship with your dad</u>, simply thank God for this amazing blessing, and that God would heal those families who don't have such a relationship:

> Dear God: I thank you that my dad and I have/had such a remarkable relationship. Please heal the hearts of those families who haven't experienced such a relationship. Amen.

CHAPTER 5 QUESTIONS:

1. Did your dad have any "Man Rules" and, if so, what were they?
2. Why is it so important to remember that we have a heavenly Father who NEVER makes mistakes, who ALWAYS loves us, who NEVER forsakes us?
3. Consider **CHALLENGE #5**: Based on your situation, how will you be able to meet this challenge?

6

I FORGIVE YOU, DAD
(BECAUSE JESUS FORGIVES)

"For if you forgive other people when they sin against you, your heavenly Father will also forgive you. But if you do not forgive others their sins, your Father will not forgive your sins."

MATTHEW 6:14-15 (NIV)

"Not forgiving someone is like drinking poison and expecting the other person to die."

~ UNKNOWN

HAVING REALIZED THAT, to varying degrees, all of us suffer from our own fathers' sins against us, we begin with an often uncomfortable, but necessary, act of will: forgiving Dad.

Forgiveness is defined as the act of ending anger against someone. This is a conscious act of our will, not something we need to wait to do until the stars and planets align. Instead we must courageously proclaim: I forgive you, Dad. After all, it's usually easier to hang onto unforgiveness than to simply forgive. Why is that? Here are a few reasons:

- **It's comfortable**: For starters, unforgiveness can seem to be a place of comfort to us. But I would argue that it's actually more likely a discomfort to us, because we've confused unforgiveness for peace.
- **It's a "leg-up"**: Unforgiveness also gives us a "leg-up", a bargaining chip over the person who wronged us, in this case, our dads. We often feel like we've got something over on the person who took advantage of us, and we're hesitant to release that "power" we perceive we have.
- **A holier-than-thou attitude**: Our forgiveness can sometimes be propelled by our own holier-than-thou attitude, a suffocating air of moral superiority we feel we deserve: we'd *never* act in such a way as dad did to me.
- **We're angry**: Our unforgiveness is a smoldering ember of fury – how *dare* my father treat me like that? We may even hate our father for what he's done to us. But, as my bride often relates, hate is simply love disappointed. We find it easier to be angry at dad rather than to simply forgive him.
- **We're hurt:** This gets to the heart of the issue. The vulnerability we felt about our dad may be better protected now that we're mature adults, but we remain vulnerable to dad's lack of both love and compassion in our own lives. Many men resolve to never let somebody that close to them hurt them that badly again. It's just too painful; we never want to remember the way that made us feel. Forgiving them, in many of our minds, just justifies wrong behavior.
- **We can't get it back**: That idyllic childhood we wanted? That perfect camping trip we always dreamed about? That time alone fishing or hunting with dad that never happened? Gone! Like spilt milk or a fair balloon carelessly released to the sky, many of us men have the real feeling that nothing will ever replace what dad took from us, or never gave to us in the first place.
- **We need someone to blame:** Face it: it's a lot easier and more convenient if I have someone to blame for the shortcomings in

my own life. No, men won't likely come out and say this, because many of us don't even know we do it. But it's far easier for me to blame my upbringing – Dad was never there for me – than to blame myself. It's far more difficult to take responsibility for my actions than to simply blame my dad because he didn't set a good example. *How could I be at fault?*

From the theme of our guide from 1 Corinthians 11:1, "Follow my example, as I follow the example of Christ", we turn to the classic forgiveness lessons from Jesus' Parable of the Unmerciful Servant of Matthew 18:21-35 (NIV):

The Parable of the Unmerciful Servant (Matthew 18:21-35)

²¹Then Peter came to Jesus and asked, "Lord, how many times shall I forgive my brother when he sins against me? Up to seven times?"
²²Jesus answered, "I tell you, not seven times, but seventy-seven times.
²³"Therefore, the kingdom of heaven is like a king who wanted to settle accounts with his servants. ²⁴As he began the settlement, a man who owed him ten thousand talents was brought to him. ²⁵Since he was not able to pay, the master ordered that he and his wife and his children and all that he had be sold to repay the debt.
²⁶"The servant fell on his knees before him. 'Be patient with me,' he begged, 'and I will pay back everything.' ²⁷The servant's master took pity on him, canceled the debt and let him go.
²⁸"But when that servant went out, he found one of his fellow servants who owed him a hundred denarii. He grabbed him and began to choke him. 'Pay back what you owe me!' he demanded.
²⁹"His fellow servant fell to his knees and begged him, 'Be patient with me, and I will pay you back.'
³⁰"But he refused. Instead, he went off and had the man thrown into prison until he could pay the debt. ³¹When the other servants saw what had happened, they were greatly distressed and went and told their master everything that had happened.

[32]"Then the master called the servant in. 'You wicked servant,' he said, 'I canceled all that debt of yours because you begged me to. [33]Shouldn't you have had mercy on your fellow servant just as I had on you?' [34]In anger his master turned him over to the jailers to be tortured, until he should pay back all he owed.

[35]"This is how my heavenly Father will treat each of you unless you forgive your brother from your heart." Matthew 18:21-35 (NIV)

As we consider forgiving our own father, Jesus has much to teach us through this parable:

- **There are no limits on the number of times we're to forgive** (Matthew 18:21-22) – As Jesus and Peter discuss the number of times we're to forgive someone, Jesus answers seventy-seven times. In fact, some translators indicate not seventy-seven times but "7 x 70" or 490 times. Regardless of the actual numerical result, the net result is the same: there are no boundaries on the number of times we're to forgive. Not to put too fine a point on it: God commands us to forgive everyone, even our own father, regardless of how many times he's wronged us.

- **God has forgiven us much** (Matthew 18:23-27) – This parable's main character, the unmerciful servant, amassed a debt of 10,000 talents, the equivalent of millions of dollars – quite a liability! Yet, falling to his knees, he begged the king to show mercy. And the king did! Better yet, instead of reducing his entire family to servitude or even killing him out of anger, the king took pity on his begging, debt-laden servant. The parallel here is, of course, God has forgiven us, not 10,000 talents, but much more – all of our sins, every one of them! We are in His debt for what Jesus paid for us on Calvary's cross.

- **We often see ourselves in the unforgiving servant** (Matthew 18:28-30) – If the parable simply ended before this point, it would have been a joyous story, but the best lessons are yet to come. The unforgiving servant, having been forgiven the equivalent of millions of dollars of debt, now runs out and tries to exact his own debt repayment plan to recoup "a hundred denarii", the equivalent of a few dollars. So, to properly frame this, this same servant who had been forgiven millions of dollars was now scrounging for a few dollars another servant owed him. And, in this, we see ourselves in the unforgiving servant. That's embarrassing and shameful to us.

- **Our wickedness is often known by others** (Matthew 18:31) – What's even more embarrassing to us is that, when we're caught in sin, oftentimes others are aware of our sins. Specifically, when we refuse to forgive our dad, it's not just we who are affected – others know about it, too. Here I am, trying to just get by in privately not forgiving my dad, and others know about it. Are you willing to think through who might also know about your refusal to forgive your own dad?

- **Refusing to forgive others is wicked** (Matthew 18:32-33) – The king, represented by Jesus Himself, doesn't mince words calling the unmerciful servant, "You wicked, lazy servant…." The lesson is clear: refusing to forgive others is wicked. Specifically, refusing to forgive your own father is wicked. That's a harsh reality to be confronted with, one that makes me feel very uncomfortable. That's the Holy Spirit nudging you into righteousness.

- **There are dire consequences if we don't forgive others** (Matthew 18:35) – And here's where the rubber hits the road: forgive others… or else. This isn't an ultimatum over which we have no choice: forgiveness is always a choice. I would argue that if we wait for the perfect time, the perfect occasion, the perfect set-up to forgive someone, we would wait forever; that time will not arrive. Forgive your dad before it's too late.

- **In summation, God has forgiven us, so He expects us to forgive others** – God has forgiven us much (that is millions of dollars) and He, therefore, expects us to forgive little (a few dollars), each and every time a person wrongs, or sins, against us. The path forward is clear: forgive because God forgave you.

Now arrives the delicate task of tying together this parable to the relationship I had with my own dad. As you know from my earlier descriptions, I had a really good dad, a dad who loved being a dad, a dad who loved his bride, and a dad who loved his family. Yet, despite that fantastic undergirding of an excellent parental support system, I, embarrassingly, experienced disappointment in my own father's passing.

The initial disappointment was largely due to the fact that my father was relatively young when he passed – he perished at 63, though he had been suffering memory loss in his late 50's. Over and over I would pray to God about Dad, "Dear Lord, please heal Dad here on earth…or perfectly in heaven." Man, I prayed that prayer like the rosary – over and over again, in many different locations, different times of day, and different states of mind. Now, God, being God, was supposed to know that when I prayed that prayer, what I REALLY wanted was for God to heal Dad here on earth. You see, I thought it polite, and was more than a little proud of myself that I had given God an option: either heal Dad here on earth, or perfectly in heaven. We're supposed to give God options, right? Yet, as it became clear that God was not going to heal Dad on earth, my disappointment, which began as a low grade fever, gradually heated up to a full-blown challenge to my faith: Why would God do this to Dad? More selfishly, why would God do this to *me*? In other words, I was disappointed in God for choosing to take Dad home so soon, so early, before he could even look upon his grandkids graduating from high school, or his future great grandkids. It all seemed so unfair.

If that wasn't alarming enough, my disappointment in seeing Dad pass so early was related to another painful reality: I didn't want Dad to leave me. In the years and months before Dad's passing, I would wake up in the middle of the night, crying over my dad. It wasn't that I was experiencing nightmares – just the opposite. Often times in my dreams, Dad and I would be walking in the woods, spending time with Mom, and our family – all normal stuff. Yet, even in my dreams, I knew Dad was leaving us. So painful was that loss, that I found I was engaging in the thoroughly scandalous exercise of not forgiving Dad for the things I perceived he had done to me through the years: he joked that my 9th grade hair style made me look like I belonged in a barber-shop quartet; he made me play saxophone; he refused to watch or let us play baseball. So, here God has given me what I, and many others, consider to be a model father, and yet, as my dad's passing loomed, then arrived, and then became a memory, I subconsciously kept finding fault in the way he raised me. "Dad could have done this better! Dad should have done this better!" I stormed in my mind. It was several painful years later that the Holy Spirit reckoned with me: I was holding my dear dad to a much higher standard than I myself would have wanted to be held to. Hold on, there's more. The Holy Spirit revealed to me that I was a coward: holding onto unforgiveness and "cutting my dad down to size" were my ill-fated grief coping mechanisms to lessen the sting of losing my dad. Sin! You see, in my abject and twisted grief, if I could somehow lessen my dad in my own eyes, well then I wouldn't miss him so much. Do all dads have faults? Of course! We know this! Yet, here I was, not even realizing that I was tearing down my own dad, refusing to forgive him, because of all the pain I had bottled up inside about his pending demise. Now, five years after dad's passing, I awoke again in tears, mourning my dad's passing. And, soon after, I was gripped by my own sinful tendencies to tear a good man – a faithful dad – down to my level. It was nothing less than cowardice!

Now Dad's gone and, as the Holy Spirit revealed to me soon after Dad's passing in May 2011, God was so grieved by how He saw my dad suffering that God did the most merciful act He could have ever granted Dad: God took my dad home to be with Him. Dad no longer suffers from memory loss, no longer trudges around in a half-full diaper, no longer cries uncontrollably as he was ripped away from his home. Dad continually celebrates with Jesus forevermore. As it turns out, God answered my prayer request *exactly*, beyond my wildest dreams for Dad's best provision.

Yet, here I stand with the choice of healing forgiveness…or tormenting, persistent unforgiveness. Are you a little like me? Is your unforgiveness wearing you down, too?

In my situation, I can no longer approach my own dad to ask for his forgiveness – Dad's earthly body is dead, but he has been taken into the Lord's presence. So, Dad's gone, and the reasonable question arises: Can there be one-sided forgiveness? The answer is YES, and here are a couple examples found in Scripture:

- Jesus cried aloud from the cross in Luke 23:34 (NLT), "Father, forgive them for they do not know what they are doing."
- Stephen, as he was also being martyred through stoning in Acts 7:60 (ESV), "Lord, do not hold this sin against them."

Whether your father is alive or no longer living, God calls us to forgive him, just as He has forgiven us.

So, "Follow my example, as I follow the example of Christ" by forgiving your dad.

CHALLENGE #6: If there is a need, forgive your dad, remembering God forgives us.

Dear God, please help me forgive my father for the things he's done against me, both intentional and unintentional sins. Help me forgive dad as You've forgiven me for the things I've done against You, both intentional and unintentional sins. Amen.

OR

If there is/was a spirit of forgiveness between you and your dad simply praise God for this blessing.

Dear God, I praise you for the spirit of forgiveness you've blessed Dad and me with. Please help other families experience this blessing as well. Amen.

CHAPTER 6 QUESTIONS:

1. Why is it usually easier to hang onto unforgiveness than to simply forgive?
2. How would you sum up Jesus' The Parable of the Unmerciful Servant (Matthew 18:21-35)?
3. Consider **CHALLENGE #6**: Based on your situation, how will you be able to meet this challenge?

7

PEACE, DAD (BECAUSE JESUS RECONCILED WITH US)

For God was pleased to have all his fullness dwell in him
[Christ], and through him to reconcile to himself all things,
whether things on earth or things in heaven, by making
peace through his blood, shed on the cross.

COLOSSIANS 1:19-20 (NIV)

"Christian faith is…basically about love and reconciliation.
These things are so important, they're foundational and they
transform individuals, families."

PHILIP YANCEY

THE SALVIA IN my mouth evaporated as if I had consumed three cups of coffee, and it was now drier than a sun baked attic. Yet, my palms glistened with moisture and I unconsciously rubbed them together as if to dispel not just the sweat, by my discomfort as well. Dad had agreed to hear my complaint in the setting of our family cabin.

After harboring a particular complaint against my dad, and having repeatedly taken it to the Lord in prayer, I sensed the Holy Spirit guiding me to set up a time to talk man-to-man with my dad. Now, in my family, we rarely discussed conflict. If there was conflict you swept it under the rug and moved on. So, to contact my dad and then discuss it with him was not in the Zimmerman protocol. Nonetheless, Dad agreed to hear me out and, one summer Saturday afternoon, Dad and I sat down to talk. Jittery, my heart racing, I calmly laid out the issue in under 30 seconds. Dad listened patiently, thought about it, and then expressed a heartfelt apology. It was one of the most awkward, yet solidifying encounters I had ever had with Dad. The lesson to me that day was simple: listen to the Holy Spirit, even when you feel uncomfortable. After that, the issue never came up again between Dad and me.

Dad and I had reconciled.

After we make a deliberate choice and forgive our dads, we are now ready for the next step, an equally challenging but rewarding act: reconciling with them. In short, peace, Dad.

WHY CAN RECONCILIATION BE SO DIFFICULT?

A simple definition of reconciliation is the process of restoring a broken relationship. We've forgiven the offender; now the challenge is to rebuild the relationship with him. As you would expect, reconciliation can be difficult. But why?

FACTORS IN RECONCILIATION

There are several factors in reconciliation:

- **The attitude of the people involved** – If either you or your dad, or both of you, enter the reconciliation discussion with little hope in God's restorative abilities, the process will take much longer, if indeed it happens at all.

- **Repeated behavior** – You've been down the path of reconciliation, but then either you or your dad hit a snag and a long-held stumbling block derails you. But it's not the first time, and the thought creeps in: When will this behavior truly stop?
- **The severity of the act** – Many small actions can paint a broader picture of the overall relationship; but often a single act, such as divorcing your mom or striking you physically, can be so severe that it seems beyond forgiveness, much less reconciliation.

RECONCILIATION IS A PROCESS

Truly, these factors play a role in how well, or how poorly, reconciliation goes. But remember: reconciliation is less of a one-time act than it is a process:

- It may take years;
- it may be erratic; and
- both you and your dad may become impatient with one another.

RECONCILIATION IMPOSSIBLE?

But is reconciliation ever impossible? Sadly, yes. Remember, forgiveness and reconciliation are not the same thing. Forgiveness is the act of ending anger at someone; reconciliation is restoring a broken relationship. Forgiveness is a repeated, willful act that can be done solo; reconciliation is a process that requires two people working together towards restoring mutual peace.

Here I share several examples where reconciliation ranges from not yet possible to impossible:

- **We never see each other** – Long-distance relationships can work, and I'm not talking about Grease's "Summer Nights." I have several friends I haven't seen in a decade although I regularly keep up with them, but reconciliation with an old boss of mine probably won't happen because we never see each other, and the boss is likely unaware that something is wrong between us.

- **They're too angry with me** – In a different kind of situation, the person you're trying to reconcile with might be so upset with you that, at this point, reconciliation isn't yet possible. You've forgiven them, but they haven't yet forgiven you. For example, as much as I would like to reconcile with an old business partner of mine whom I've forgiven, I cannot approach him because he is upset with me – he mistakenly holds me responsible for running his business into the ground. Working in him despite his anger is something that only the Holy Spirit do. Until then, I can pray. And so can you.
- **This person is dead** – In my view, this is the most troublesome of the reconciliation barriers – the person is dead. God gave me an opportunity to reconcile with my dad, but many of us won't have that chance because our dad has passed on. This doesn't mean that peace isn't possible; it just means healing that personal relationship isn't possible. Remember, forgiveness is something we're always in control of (Mark 11:25), and it always leads to peace (Colossians 3:15), something else we're in control of.

So, the difficult lesson is that reconciliation isn't always possible. However, it remains a goal and a desired effect for many of us. If it's possible, reconciliation with our dad remains a noble, sometimes elusive, always rewarding goal.

ACTIONS ALWAYS TRUMP WORDS

American statesman and inventor Ben Franklin quipped, "Well done is better than well said." Jesus Himself instructed in Matthew 7:16 (BLB), "by their fruits you will recognize them." Similarly, working through reconciliation will always be better than simply talking about it.

WE ARE IMPERFECT

God is perfect; we are not. God does not sin; we do – every day. Therefore, our motives and actions arise from our sinful nature and thus can be skewed. Our love, forgiveness, and reconciliation are, accordingly, imperfect, conditional:

- I'll love him IF he treats me this way; or
- I'll forgive him IF he apologizes for what he did to me; or
- I'll reconcile with him IF he repents of his sin.

Because we're human, each one of us has a natural tendency to place such conditions on personal situations, especially if we've been hurt in the past. But God's love is UNCONDITIONAL – it's irrespective of who we are, how we think, or what we do (think John 3:16). So in reconciling with our dad, we honor God by setting aside our conditions and instead let His unconditional grace work through any trouble we encounter. Jesus offers an excellent example of reconciliation in the Sermon on the Mount.

Key lessons on reconciliation from Jesus' Sermon on the Mount (Matthew 5:23-26)

[23]"Therefore, if you are offering your gift at the altar and there remember that your brother has something against you, [24]leave your gift there in front of the altar. First go and be reconciled to your brother; then come and offer your gift.
[25]"Settle matters quickly with your adversary who is taking you to court. Do it while you are still with him on the way, or he may hand you over to the judge, and the judge may hand you over to the officer, and you may be thrown into prison. [26]I tell you the truth, you will not get out until you have paid the last penny.
Matthew 5:23-26 (NIV)

As we consider reconciling with our own father, Jesus provides much to consider:

- **Reconciliation comes before offering** (Matthew 5:23-24) – The offering is a vital component of worship, but Jesus teaches that settling up on matters of the heart precedes an offering in both worship practice and priority. Jesus further teaches in Matthew 9:13 (BSB), "But go and learn what this means: 'I desire mercy, not sacrifice...'"

So urgent is the manner of reconciliation that Jesus encouraged His followers to put their offering on hold and go make it right with the brother they've offended.

- **God commands us to be reconciled with each person** (Matthew 5:24) – the brother Jesus speaks of in this verse can be considered not just our actual brother but any person, including our dad.

- **God commands us to reconciled to our enemies** (Matthew 5:25) – It turns out Jesus teaches us to be reconciled with all people, including our enemies. Sadly, this might also include your own dad, but as we are emphasizing here, the goal is to make peace with Dad.

- **There are dire consequences if we don't reconcile with others when we're able to** (Matthew 5:26) – The person who refused to reconcile in this story landed in jail. And, while it's difficult for us to imagine doing time for not reconciling with our dad, many of us can attest that not reconciling with our dad is somewhat like a prison sentence: we have doubt, worry, and may even feel trapped. We can infer from Jesus' teachings that "jail time" is a totally avoidable consequence.

- **To sum up, reconciliation with both friends and enemies is what God commands** – God knows best and, as challenging as this teaching is, we can always trust His ways.

Thus, the relationship between this Sermon on the Mount lesson and our own dad is two-fold:

- **Peace with God:** To follow Christ is to seek peace – to reconcile – with our dad the best we can. We have no idea how our prayers will affect a change, but we know only God can change hearts. Agreeing in prayer with Him leads to the best result possible: peace with God.

- **Love like Christ:** Reconciliation, while often difficult, remains an opportunity for us to continue to pray for our dads who refuse to make peace with us. It's a chance to love them like Christ. This is undoubtedly one of the most heart-wrenching aspects of our walk with Christ: dropping our armor (pride, hurt, disappointment) and reconciling in peace with dad.

We've defined what reconciliation is, discussed why reconciliation can be so difficult, and learned from Jesus some key lessons on reconciliation and how they relate to our relationship with our own dad. It can be a painful exercise to enter into, but we can trust God that He will be working in the midst of this process called reconciliation. Again, we can reconcile because Jesus set the model for reconciliation.

Follow my example, as I follow the example of Christ…by reconciling, if possible, with your dad.

CHALLENGE #7: If a need exists, reconcile with your father if possible, remembering God has reconciled with His children.

OR

If you and your father have already reconciled or if reconciliation is impossible, ask God to help other fathers and sons reconcile.

CHAPTER 7 QUESTIONS:

1. Why can reconciliation be so difficult?
2. What are some similarities and differences between forgiveness and reconciliation?
3. Consider **CHALLENGE #7**: Based on your situation, how will you be able to meet this challenge?

8

THANKS, DAD (BECAUSE JESUS ENCOURAGES THANKFULNESS)

After the stone had been rolled aside, Jesus looked up toward heaven and prayed, "Father, I thank you for answering my prayer. I know that you always answer my prayers. But I said this, so that the people here would believe that you sent me."

JOHN 11:41-42 (CEV)

"When I was a boy of fourteen, my father was so ignorant I could hardly stand to have the old man around. But when I got to be twenty-one, I was astonished at how much he had learned in seven years."

~ MARK TWAIN

IN THE BEST case scenario, we've forgiven our father and we're working towards reconciliation, so a natural next step is to thank him. Ironically, thanking him is an exercise that will aid in our efforts to continue both forgiving and seeking peace with Dad.

A straightforward definition of thankfulness is a feeling or expression of gratitude. For many of us, it seems to be pretty routine to express our appreciation:

- Thanks for your service to our country.
- Thanks for the ride.
- Thanks for saving me a seat.

But, when it comes to thanking our loved ones, many of us find that we stumble. So why do we sometimes turn aside from thanking others? Here are a few reasons you may identify with:

- **It's awkward** – It can be awkward to thank someone we've been either physically or emotionally separated from and whom we barely think we know.
- **It's an unjust reward** – We may feel thanking someone validates his otherwise poor behavior.
- **My pride** – Our pride gets in the way. Need I say more?
- **Their pride** – We may think that thanking someone will cause the other person's pride to swell.
- **Not worthy** – We may think they don't deserve gratitude, because of what the person did.
- **My embarrassment** – We may be embarrassed that the act we're thanking them for is not an act we would have done. For example, it could be embarrassing to thank dad for giving up every Saturday for your childhood swim practices if you aren't willing to do that for your own kids.
- **Thanks, but no thanks** – We may feel obligated that we'll have to "return the favor."

Key lessons of thankfulness from Jesus heals ten men who have a skin disease (Luke 17:11-19 NIRV)

¹¹ Jesus was on his way to Jerusalem. He traveled along the border between Samaria and Galilee. ¹² As he was going into a village, ten men met him. They had a skin disease. They were standing close by. ¹³ And they called out in a loud voice, "Jesus! Master! Have pity on us!"

¹⁴ Jesus saw them and said, "Go. Show yourselves to the priests." While they were on the way, they were healed.

¹⁵ When one of them saw that he was healed, he came back. He praised God in a loud voice. ¹⁶ He threw himself at Jesus' feet and thanked him. The man was a Samaritan.

¹⁷ Jesus asked, "Weren't all ten healed? Where are the other nine? ¹⁸ Didn't anyone else return and give praise to God except this outsider?" ¹⁹ Then Jesus said to him, "Get up and go. Your faith has healed you." Luke 17:11-19 (NIRV)

As we consider thanking our own father, Jesus has much to teach us through this parable:

- **Each of us has needs** (Luke 17:11-13) – A crowd of men, all with the same pressing need, approached Jesus. At the time of Jesus' earthly ministry, those suffering from leprosy or other diseases of the skin were separated from society, living in leper communities. These men shared an urgent need, just as each one of us today also has urgent needs: healing, acceptance, justice among others. We can go to Jesus to tell our needs to the One who not only knows them, but also is concerned about us.

- **Jesus heals us** (Luke 17:14) – In faith, the 10 men moved out under Jesus' command, and immediately received healing. Now, like then, Jesus heals us.

- **We can thank Jesus aloud** (Luke 17:15-16) – Only one of the 10 who were healed returned, and he was a Samaritan at that! Why is this remarkable? Samaritans engaged in a religion that was a mix of both Judaism and idolatry; they were generally considered "half-breeds" despised by the

Jews. That a Samaritan would return to thank Jesus would have been an embarrassment to the Jews. Nonetheless, we are reminded of the importance of thanking Jesus aloud for what He's done for us. Sure, we may not physically throw ourselves on the ground, but the exuberance of this one man's gratitude is felt even now.

- **Many of us do not thank Jesus** (Luke 17:17-18) – With only one in 10 (10%) returning, clearly the other nine – the vast majority – did not return to praise God. So often times in my prayers, I ask God for many things, but I find myself deficient in thanking Him in at least an equal amount. Yet we have so much to be thankful for. Thinking of something to thank our dad for may take a little effort, but there are likely at least a few instances that warrant our gratitude.

- **Our faith in Jesus makes us well** (Luke 17:19) – Each of the 10 men received healing, but the only man who returned learned the truth *behind* his healing – his own faith in Jesus Christ. It was this Samaritan who learned that prized lesson, the spiritual healing! And, today, our faith in Jesus not only makes us physically well, but helps make our relationships well. Jesus heals all wounds: bodies, minds, and relationships.

- **To sum up, Jesus prizes thankfulness for God and what He is doing.**

A FATHERLY EXAMPLE OF THANKFULNESS

Years before the darkness stole into his brain and his joy for life was slowly snuffed from his consciousness, Dad would frequently bless us with verbally inspirational words, as well as words of encouragement shared through written notes. This was even more remarkable given Dad's tendency to speak even less than trees do. As a touching example, back in 2000, God had just blessed us with our second child, our first son, Koen. In between lack of sleep and burning the candle at both ends, Suzanne and I weren't able to agree on whether having the first child or the second child was more challenging. Yes, there's plenty of joyfulness, especially since we enjoy five children now.

However, having that second kid is a critical juncture, effectively *doubling* the number of kids as they pull even with you: parents – two, kids – two. Feeling more than a little overwhelmed with a two-year-old and an inconveniently awake newborn, I reached out to Dad for some fatherly advice. Swallowing my pride, I emailed Dad Mark Twain's famous saying that I quoted at the beginning of this chapter. Dad's response is a classic encouragement letter, one which I've kept to this day:

> *I'm sure you'll face the same situation in the years to come. Enjoy the years when you are everything to your children. At 12 or 13 they are ashamed to be seen with you, then at 15 or 16 they think you're stupid and out of touch. After a few months in college, they realize what they had in the good old days in high school when life was a lark, and finally they realize that your old Dad isn't such a bad guy after all. When they're married with kids of their own it is nice to experience the mutual respect you have with your children. Finally you can be friends. Up until that time you must be a father first. Sometimes it hurts to be a father and sometimes you have to keep from laughing at your kids. If they only knew how naïve they are or how foolish they are or how utterly wrong they are. But, you have to let them fail and fall down so they can learn to stand strong and finally grow up. Through it all, you never stop loving them.*
>
> *Dad*
>
> *P.S. Love to all and especially the little ones. You and Suzanne are really good parents. I have all the confidence that our grandchildren are in good hands.*

Several years ago, as I re-read this letter, I realized his encouraging words were yet another aspect of my own dad's lasting legacy. Then it occurred to me: What if I were to follow my own dad's example by expressing thanks to him?

What would that look like?

It would look like a challenge, of course!

CHALLENGE #8: If possible, contact your dad in whatever method you feel most comfortable with (written letter, phone call, text, meet for breakfast, etc.) and thank him.

OR

If not possible, write a thank you letter to your dad and share it with your family.

So, now it's our turn...

So, whether your dad is still living, whether he's passed on, or whether or not you're able to forgive him right now, you can remember a positive aspect of his legacy even now. What I wouldn't give right now to be able to see and talk to my own dad again! If your dad's still living then don't miss this chance I've challenged you with: to reach out to your dad and thank him.

To help get the process started, I've outlined some basic steps below that you can use to guide your interaction, whether it's through a letter, a phone call, a text message, or a catch-up breakfast.

1. Start with a simple greeting like, "Hi, Dad..."
2. Thank your dad for his legacy by remembering a specific example of how he impacted your life, regardless of the age you were at the time. For example:
   a. Was there a time your dad took you hunting? Thank him.
   b. Did you see your dad take a stand for something unpopular? Thank him.
   c. How did your dad inspire you? Thank him.
   d. When did your dad protect you? Thank him.
   e. What did your dad sacrifice for you? Thank him.
   f. Did your dad strive for something good? Thank him.

    g. Why was your dad passionate about something admirable? Thank him.

    h. What good example did your dad set for you to follow? Thank him.

3. Briefly explain/write to your dad why you love him (even if he's no longer here). For example, "Dad, I love you, because you spent time with me."

4. Review your approach with your family, noting their reaction.

5. Next, pray together with your family that your dad would receive your gesture.

6. Now, share your appreciation with your dad: phone him, text him, email him, or visit him.

7. If you feel comfortable, encourage other dads by sharing your letter either publicly or anonymously with us at www.AFaithfulDad.org/thankyouletter.

Be encouraged here, Dad. Even a child (in this case, our then six-year-old, Grant) can craft a simple, but effective thank you:

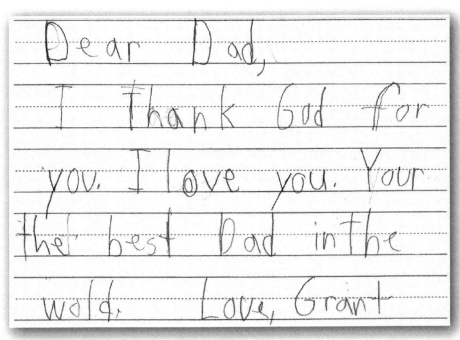

Dear Dad,
I thank God for you. I love you. Your the best Dad in the world. Love, Grant

Follow my example as I follow the example of Christ…by thanking your dad.

CHAPTER 8 QUESTIONS:

1. Why do we sometimes turn aside from thanking others?
2. How would you sum up the time when Jesus heals ten men who have a skin disease (Luke 17:11-19)?
3. Consider **CHALLENGE #8**: How will you accomplish this challenge?

PART 3

HOW DO I CARRY IT OUT?

9

LIVE FOR GOD

For me, to live is Christ and to die is gain.

PHILIPPIANS 1:21 (ESV)

"God loves each of us as if there were only one of us."

~ AUGUSTINE

LIVING FOR GOD is the heart of this guide, the cornerstone of our legacy. Yet, for most of my life, I lived not for God but for myself. Only myself. Maybe you're like me?

Disturbingly, my life, in at least one respect, eerily paralleled the 1999 thriller, M. Night Shyamalan's *The Sixth Sense*. For those who haven't seen it, I'm issuing a *** SPOILER ALERT *** right now. One of the movie's most memorable scenes features a frightening conversation between young Cole Sear (played by Haley Joel Osment) and Malcom Crowe (played by Bruce Willis):

Cole Sear: I see dead people.

Malcolm Crowe: In your dreams? [*Cole shakes his head no*]

Malcolm Crowe: While you're awake? [*Cole nods*]

Malcolm Crowe: Dead people like, in graves? In coffins?

Cole Sear: Walking around like regular people. They don't see each other. They only see what they want to see. They don't know they're dead.

Malcolm Crowe: How often do you see them?

Cole Sear: All the time. They're everywhere.

Now, brace yourself to find out how this dialogue so paralleled my own life at the time. In other words, prepare to be shocked...in a bad way.

CHURCH SHOPPING IN D.C.

It was an honor and lifelong dream to serve our country as a United States Air Force officer. As is well documented, no one in the military stays in one place for long. The years just before my bride and I had children found us serving at Randolph AFB in beautiful San Antonio, TX. So, when the time came for my bride and me to transfer, and sensing we were about to start a family, we put in our preference for the Washington, D.C. area to be close to my parents. To our delight, when the United States Air Force Personnel Center issued our official military orders in the spring of 1997, then Captain Travis and Mrs. Suzanne Zimmerman were transferred from San Antonio, TX to Washington, D.C. Incidentally, that was three years before I came back to the Lord.

Understandably, Suzanne and I were anxious to quickly integrate into the D.C. community, but we both held drastically different priorities...and motives. At the top of Suzanne's priority list was finding a church. "Yeah, me, too," I assured her. Yikes, that really wasn't anywhere *near* my top priority. In fact, it wasn't even *on* my priority list.

In deciding upon our future "D.C. church home" (as she called it), it turns out that Suzanne was looking for three absolutely crazy things from a church:

1. She held this ridiculous notion that our "church home" must be a Bible-believing, Bible-teaching church – What a nut!
2. Suzanne insisted on the preposterous concept that prayer partners and small groups were a necessity for our future church – Can you believe this woman? And lastly...
3. She clung to the ludicrous thought that we should be able to serve with others in our church and community – Outlandish rubbish! Next she'll probably start talking about tithing or washing feet or other church nonsense!

I'm telling you, to "dead" people like I was then, this was just absolutely insane, off-the-wall stuff – Why would anyone want to go to a church that meets those wacko requirements? I didn't know it then, but God certainly categorized my thinking by the Apostle Paul's writing:

For the message of the cross is foolishness to those who are perishing, but to us who are being saved it is the power of God. 1 Corinthians 1:18 (NIV)

I was foolish, and I didn't know it.

Worse, I was dead, and I didn't even know it.

Nonetheless, I "went through the motions" of looking for a "church home" that met Suzanne's requirements. But, inside my head, I harbored my own secret list of requirements – important requirements, mind you! Here's what I was looking for:

1. I thought it critically important to join a church with huge, oversized stained-glass windows. I was going to get bored at church and, if you're going to be bored at church, you might as well have some pretty stained-glass windows to look out of to take your mind off of the pastor's convicting message.
2. I was seeking a church that had plenty of Mercedes and BMWs in the parking lot. After all, if I wanted to build up my huge ego, what better way to advance my career than by making a good, real impression on people of wealth and influence? In the hummable words of Frank Sinatra, "Start spreading the news...I'm leaving today!"
3. Lastly, I wanted a huge church with a ton of people, so many people, in fact, that I could anonymously slip into – and out of – church without being noticed. No accountability, no lasting friendships, and certainly no awkward questions. Don't ask me my business, people!

It's an understatement to point out that my bride and I were a bit out of sync in our agreeing on a "church home." You see, it turns out my bride was looking for a church built on Christ; in retrospect now, there were plenty of D.C. churches of various denominations that love to serve and proclaim His name.

I, on the other hand, was searching for the "Church of Me." Though I didn't realize it until several years later, I was *never* going to find a church that would lead to lasting and meaningful results – never. Sure, I may have found a church that I thought met *my* criteria, but it wouldn't have addressed the one true fact:

I was walking around dead, and I didn't even know it.

After one particularly "frustrating" Sunday morning service – probably the fourth or fifth church we had visited that month – I remember Suzanne and I feeling totally frazzled about not being able to agree on the "right" church. So, completely exasperated, I turned to Suzanne and spouted off,

"UGH!!! How come every church we visit is so full of BROKEN people? Where are all the people who have their lives put together?"

Ah! So close, young man, yet *so* far!

Through God's perfect grace and my own bride's patient love, I eventually learned that each and every one of us is "broken," hopelessly in need of Christ's loving grace and forgiveness! It is only by the grace of our Lord Jesus Christ that we have healing, forgiveness and, of course, the real promise of life with God forever in eternity. Truly, it's about a growing relationship with Jesus Christ, our best friend, who loves us with an infinite love!

Yes, Cole Sear might as well been talking about me. Dead people – they're everywhere. I was one of them, and I didn't even know it.

Could you be one, too?

Unless you live for God and not yourself, like I was so selfishly doing, you're a dead man walking.

So let's get into that now: leave your lasting legacy by living for God.

One of my favorite New Testament passages finds Jesus engaged in one of His many debates with the religious rulers of ancient Israel; the discussion has much to say about living for God. Let's "listen in" now on one such debate found in Mark 12:28-30 (NIV):

> [28]One of the teachers of the law came and heard them debating. Noticing that Jesus had given them a good answer, he asked him, "Of all the commandments, which is the most important?" [29]**The most important one," answered Jesus, "is this: 'Hear, O Israel, the Lord our God, the Lord is one. [30]Love the Lord your God with all your heart and with all your soul and with all your mind and with all your strength.'"**

The boldfaced passages (my emphasis) are, of course, from the Shema, the Hebrew word for "hear" that begins the most important prayer in all of

Judaism. The Scripture passage Jesus references here draws from Moses' address to the Jews of the Exodus in Deuteronomy 6:4-9. Jesus teaches that of the 613 commands of Mosaic Law, loving God is *the* most important commandment: to love God wholeheartedly heart, soul, mind, and strength. Further, Jesus makes the critical connection in John 14:15 (NLT):

"If you love me, obey my commandments."

And again soon after Jesus expands in John 14:23 (NIV):

Jesus replied, "Anyone who loves me will obey my teaching. My Father will love them, and we will come to them and make our home with them."

See the connection between loving God and living for God? By obeying God's commands, we show our love for Him and God will love us and make His home with us. In other words, He will live with us! So loving God and living for God are intimately tied together!

Living for God is loving God:

- Love the Lord your God with all your HEART – the center of human emotions.
- Love the Lord your GOD with all your SOUL – the human soul is central to your person. As George McDonald notes, "You don't have a soul. You are a Soul. You have a body."
- Love the Lord your God with all your STRENGTH – not just physical strength, but with emotional and spiritual strength, too.
- Love the Lord your God with all your MIND – the battle for your mind is real, and the place where we confront the enemy most often.

To sum up, LOVE God and LIVE for God with all you've got – now *that's* a lasting legacy! I must quickly add, however, that all of this is impossible to do without the Holy Spirit. Again, this is truth and results, as Jesus said in John 14:23, when we love God: if we love Him and keep His word, He will make His home with us. When you live for God, you inspire and encourage your family to also live for God, and that lifestyle change will reverberate endlessly!

To further inspire you in our quest for a lasting legacy, history is full of examples of Christian martyrs who lived – and died – for God:

- The Apostle Peter, the lead disciple (Matthew 10:2, Mark 3:16, Luke 6:13, Acts 1:13) who initially denied Jesus (John 18:15-27), courageously stood for Christ against the ruling Jews (Acts 4:13). As tradition holds, Peter, thinking himself unworthy to be executed in the same manner as his LORD, was crucified upside down. Peter lived for God.
- Stephen (Acts 6:7 through 7:60), in his detailed and eloquent defense of his faith in Christ, was stoned to death, even praying for his tormentors' forgiveness as he faded. Stephen lived for God.
- The Apostle Paul (2 Corinthians 11:23-29) was imprisoned, flogged, exposed to death, beaten with rods, pelted with stones, shipwrecked, subjected to extreme heat and cold, and likely beheaded. And Paul was a sinner just like us. Paul lived for God.
- Muslim militants are crucifying children to terrorize their Christian parents into fleeing Iraq. Since the war began in 2003, about 12 children, many as young as 10, have been kidnapped and killed, then nailed to makeshift crosses near their homes to terrify and torment their parents. These Iraqi Christians lived for God.
- On August 28, 2015 near Aleppo, Syria, the Islamic State (IS or ISIS) tortured, mutilated, publicly raped, and beheaded 12 Christians for saying they would "never renounce Christ for Muhammed." These Syrian Christians lived for God.

So, we've demonstrated the importance of living for God in creating a lasting legacy and shared several examples of living for Him. Now it's time to look practically at living for God.

LIVING FOR GOD: HOW DO I CARRY IT OUT?

- **Worship Him**: Worship the LORD your God, and his blessing will be on your food and water. Exodus 23:25 (NIV)
  - Put God first in *everything* you do: your personal life, your professional life, your free time. That necessarily means prioritizing all other aspects of our life behind our priority to God. Remember, while God desires that we choose Him first, He will not force His way into our lives – He will not compel you to love Him. Worship Him willingly and rejoice in all that He'll show you as you lead your family.
  - Here's an easy one: model servant leadership by taking your family to church each week. Dads, our families look to us to establish both the practice and pattern of regular corporate (i.e., attending church) worship. If you're just starting out to worship as a family, it's fine to church shop, but don't over-think it: find a church your family senses God collectively calling you to and plug in: worship, pray, serve and grow in Christ.
  - We can worship Him through our relationships, for He created each of us in His image (Genesis 1:27). Formal settings are established ways to worship Him, but also highlight for your family the beauty of God's majesty. Admiring brilliant sunrises, breathtaking sunsets, and gorgeous landscapes together are just a few of many ways we can worship Him with our family.
- **Pray to Him** (1 Thessalonians 5:17) – prayer is simply talking to God. Invite Him into your family, your conversations, your doubts, your dreams.
  - Pray as you rise each day. I pray a simple prayer when I wake each day, "Thank You for this day, Lord. Thank You for letting me live another day in Your glory. You didn't call me home yet, because You have a mission for me: to share Your

love with others. Use me today for Your purpose and Your glory. Amen"

- Pray at meals with your family. Again, dads, our families are looking for us to lead in this area. Your schedule may only allow you to pray at dinner, but don't miss this ideal opportunity to regularly bless a family meal as God blesses you.
- Pray continually for your family – sometimes I'll pray long family prayers, but mostly I'm engaged in "popcorn" prayers:
  - "Lord, please heal my bride from her constant pain and grant her the patience as we wait."
  - "May Trey's jazz band practice today bring You glory, Lord."
  - "Braden's dealing with a difficult person; please give him Your grace."
  - "God, please help my family sense Your presence today."
  - "Jesus, I'm worried about how this proposal is going to be received. May it bring glory to You today, even if it's initially rejected."
- **Evangelize to others** (Matthew 28:18-19) – The Great Commission is Jesus' call to His followers to share the Good News with a world that so desperately needs Him. There are so many ways to do this:
  - Go and make disciples by telling them what God has done. Dads, in most cases, the most readily available disciples Jesus speaks of are our own family members! A simple way to evangelize to others is to encourage them to read the Gospel of Mark because, of all the Gospels, it deals not so much with what Jesus *said* but what He *did*.
  - Evangelize in Haiti or Peru or even in your own neighborhood, but evangelize together as a family (1 Peter 2:12). And the old saying applies, "Don't export what you haven't imported." In other words, watch how you live your life: your family is watching. Ralph Waldo Emerson nailed it, "What you do speaks so loudly I cannot hear what you say."

- Tell your family and others what God has done for you – I once had a mentor encourage me to share my personal testimony, because skeptics may doubt God's Word, but they certainly can't deny the miracles God has clearly done in your own life.
- **Spend time with Him** (Psalm 42:1-2) – put simply, this is your "quiet time" with God. But how can a dad do this when a dad's life is so busy? Here are some ideas:
  - **Make it daily** – We dads are far busier than we'd admit, probably far busier than we'd ever imagined we'd be. I'm not here to beat dads up, but to empathize with you: I know that kids get sick, wives need help, boss's need status updates, and late night football games go into overtime. Yeah, we can always make an excuse, but, as many will attest, our day just seems to go better when we spend daily time with Him. Remember, our faith in Christ is a relationship that grows day-by-day. God already knows you perfectly, so spend time each day getting to know Him a little better. Regardless whether it's morning, noon, or night, make a date with God and keep it.
  - **Make it simple** – Daily reading plans are a good way to go, reading three to four chapters each day to finish God's Word in about a year. Long, uninterrupted passages of Scripture are wonderful to take in, but more easily read on a non-work day. During the work week, your reading may be as little as one chapter or even one verse. Remember, it's not the ground you cover, but being grounded in God's Word that matters, regardless of the time it takes to complete it.
  - **Take your family with you** – Whether once a day, week, or month, reading God's Word aloud to your kids and helping them better understand the Scriptures is a remarkably powerful tool God provides for us. We simply cannot underestimate how impactful it is for our family to see us dads taking leadership through Bible reading and devotionals. Keep the reading short, the discussion open, and close in short prayer as you conclude. Remember, you are leaving a lasting legacy

for God's glory! And, as you'll note below, that family encouragement is contagious; nine-year-old Elizabeth encouraged me to read Psalm 57. Priceless!

A beautiful, daughterly reminder!

- **Trust Him** (Proverbs 3:5-6) – living for God also involves trusting Him, even when you can't see the outcome.
  - **Follow Him** – God will never lead you where He has not gone before you. The same God that led Abraham to the Promised Land still leads dads today; follow Him. But from a pragmatic standpoint, keep in mind the folksy advice of

retired General Billy J. Boles, a Texas native: "Whenever you're riding point, be sure to look back every now and again to see if the herd is still following you." You're riding point, Dad, make sure your family's still following you.

- **Walk on water to Him** – Startled by seeing Jesus walking on the water (Matthew 14:22-33), the Apostle Peter initially trusts Christ, asking Jesus to call him. Consenting, Jesus watches as Peter walks on the water towards Him, but Peter sees the wind and storm and begins to sink, crying out for help. Peter's trust falters. We know the story, but Jesus also asks us to trust Him, even to walk on the water to Him. Dads, Jesus may not physically call you out on the water, but He's assuredly going to call you to do something uncomfortable, something inconvenient, and something awkward: be sure to share the details of your "water walk" with your family.
- **He's got your best interests in mind** – Remember, God knows you, wants the best for you, and has His eye on you, so don't be scared to trust Him (Romans 8:28). It's a straight-forward lesson to teach your family, dads: Just as I (Dad) have my family's best interests in mind, how much more does God have *your* best interests in mind? Always!

- **Listen to Him** (Luke 9:35) – Listening to Him seems easy at the outset, but taking the Holy Spirit's prompting and then putting it into gear is something I've grappled with through the years.
  - **Through His Word** – I hear Him most frequently while reading and meditating on His Word – Remember, God's Word will never contradict itself. Read His Word, expecting Him to speak through it. When God reveals an insight or His will, be sure to share this with your family. You'll often find your sharing will spark your family to share their own God-inspired insights.
  - **The Holy Spirit quietly whispers** – Oftentimes, I will get the distinct sense that God is speaking to me. As one of my buddies quips, "If you have to ask yourself the question

(of whether or not God is speaking to you) then you already know the answer...." Many times this is God prompting me to apologize to my bride for something ugly I've said to her, or because I totally blew a parenting call with one of my kids. As you make things right, be sure to share the specifics of how God got your attention to make things right.

- **How can I discern His voice** – This is the tough part, right? Wrong. I share a riveting example of this in Chapter 12. Again, the Holy Spirit's guidance to you will *never* contradict God's Word, the Bible. If it does, you can be certain you're *not* hearing from God. This is a reminder that Satan is also trying his worst to influence you and your family, so be sure to warn your family on how to exercise spiritual discernment here by obeying only His Word

Living for God: Our common sense tells us there's really no other way to live. Our common experience, on the other hand, shows us that this is no easy task. Yet, it's the most exhilarating way of life you could ever imagine. Go there with God, and lead your family in the Way.

Are you ready to live for God and lead your family?

CHALLENGE #9: Consider: What change(s) do you need to make to better live for God? Start today!

CHAPTER 9 QUESTIONS:

1. Do you know any "dead men walking" and could you be one of them?
2. In living for God, what's at least one practical way you can carry it out?
3. Consider **CHALLENGE #9:** What change(s) do you need to make to better live for God?

10

LIVE FOR OTHERS

"A new command I give you: Love one another. As I have loved you, so you must love one another. By this everyone will know that you are my disciples, if you love one another."

JOHN 13:34-35 (NIV)

"Do all the good you can. By all the means you can. In all the ways you can. In all the places you can. At all the times you can. To all the people you can. As long as ever you can."

~ JOHN WESLEY

GENERAL WILLIAM BOOTH, the British Methodist preacher who founded The Salvation Army, devoted his life to Christian outreach through humanitarian aid. As his productive and impactful life drew near its close and his eyesight failed him, General Booth became an invalid. So poor was his health at this point that he was unable to attend the annual Salvation

Army Convention in London, England, so one of his supporters suggested the good general dispatch a telegram message to kick off the convention. General Booth agreed.

When the thousands of delegates met, the moderator announced that General Booth would not be present because of his failing health and eyesight. Gloom and pessimism swept across the convention floor. A little light dispelled the darkness when the moderator announced that General Booth had sent a message to be read with the opening of the first session. He opened the message and began to read the following:

Dear Delegates of the Salvation Army Convention:

OTHERS!

Signed,

General Booth

Brief. Focused. Selfless. Well played, General!

As we've demonstrated, living for God is not only the most important of the 613 commands of Mosaic Law, but it's the centerpiece of leaving a lasting legacy. And, since each of us is created in God's image (Genesis 1:27), it's pretty easy to see how living for others holds the position of the second most important commandment. Again, Jesus affirms this for us in Mark 12:28-31 (NIV) by referencing the Shema:

> [28]One of the teachers of the law came and heard them debating. Noticing that Jesus had given them a good answer, he asked him, "Of all the commandments, which is the most important?" [29]"The most important one," answered Jesus, "is this: 'Hear, O Israel, the Lord our God, the Lord is one. [30]Love the Lord your God with all your

heart and with all your soul and with all your mind and with all your strength.' **³¹The second is this: 'Love your neighbor as yourself.'** There is no commandment greater than these."

There are no commandments greater than loving God and loving your neighbor, which I'll broadly designate as loving others. Just as we love God in the way we live, we also demonstrate our love for others in the way we live – as self-centric or others-centric.

LIVING FOR OTHERS IS LOVING OTHERS.
For me, and a lot of the men I talk and interact with, we definitely "get" the loving God bit. It's not that any of us does it particularly well, but we almost inherently understand the necessity of having a growing walk with God.

The loving others, part, however, makes many of us stumble, especially when we consider who "OTHERS" really are. So, who are some of the "OTHERS" God refers to?

- **Political affiliation** – From Democrat to Republican to Libertarian to the Green Party or the Tea Party, the "others" certainly make up the class we're called to love. You mean I have to love the _____ (insert political party here)? Yep.
- **Nationality** – Whether an American, Canadian, Saudi, Aussie, or South Afrikaner, God calls us to love each one. As the children's song go, "Jesus loves the little children, all the children of the world. Red, brown, yellow, black and white, they are precious in His sight. Jesus loves the little children of the world." We are those children, and because Jesus loves all children, we are to love all children, too.
- **Different religious beliefs** – God calls us to love Baptists, Methodists, Seventh Day Adventists as well as Muslims, Jews, Buddhists, and even atheists.
- **Mothers-in-Law** – Need I say more?

- **My Family** – This aspect of loving others may be easy to grasp, but hard to pull off. We will devote a good amount of this chapter to loving and living for our family.

Jesus plainly taught this concept of loving others in Luke 6:32-36 (HCSB):

[32] If you love those who love you, what credit is that to you? Even sinners love those who love them. [33] If you do what is good to those who are good to you, what credit is that to you? Even sinners do that. [34] And if you lend to those from whom you expect to receive, what credit is that to you? Even sinners lend to sinners to be repaid in full. [35] But love your enemies, do what is good, and lend, expecting nothing in return. Then your reward will be great, and you will be sons of the Most High. For He is gracious to the ungrateful and evil. [36] Be merciful, just as your Father also is merciful.

Then, as now, Jesus makes it evident that we are to love even those who don't love us, enemies in some cases. Remember, our lasting legacy is built upon how we love and live for others.

Fortunately, history is full of men who lived their lives for others:

- **John Cooper, two-time Congressional Medal of Honor winner** - On board the U.S.S. Brooklyn during action against rebel forts and gunboats and with the ram Tennessee, in Mobile Bay, 5 August 1864. Despite severe damage to his ship and the loss of several men on board as enemy fire raked her decks from stem to stern, Cooper fought his gun with skill and courage throughout the furious battle; which resulted in the surrender of the prize rebel ram Tennessee and in the damaging and destruction of batteries at Fort Morgan. **SECOND AWARD** - Served as quartermaster on Acting Rear Admiral Thatcher's staff. During the terrific fire at Mobile, on 26 April 1865, at the risk of being blown to pieces by exploding shells,

Cooper advanced through the burning locality, rescued a wounded man from certain death, and bore him on his back to a place of safety. John Cooper disregarded danger, lived for others, so allowing others to live.

- **Dietrich Bonhoeffer, German pastor, theologian, anti-Nazi dissident** - His writings on Christianity's role in the secular world have become widely influential, and his book *The Cost of Discipleship* became a modern classic. Apart from his theological writings, Bonhoeffer was known for his staunch resistance to the Nazi dictatorship, including vocal opposition to Hitler's euthanasia program and genocidal persecution of the Jews. He was arrested in April 1943 by the Gestapo and imprisoned at Tegel prison for one and a half years. Later he was transferred to a Nazi concentration camp. After being associated with the plot to assassinate Adolf Hitler, he was quickly tried, along with other accused plotters, including former members of the *Abwehr* (the German Military Intelligence Office), and then executed by hanging on 9 April 1945 as the Nazi regime was collapsing. Dietrich Bonhoeffer courageously spoke out against anti-Semitism though his passion for others cost him his own life.

- **Nelson Mandela, the South African anti-apartheid revolutionary, politician, and philanthropist** - Served as President of South Africa from 1994 to 1999. He was the country's first black chief executive, and the first elected in a fully representative democratic election. His government focused on dismantling the legacy of apartheid through tackling institutionalized racism and fostering racial reconciliation. Politically an African nationalist and democratic socialist, he served as President of the African National Congress (ANC) party from 1991 to 1997. Not even imprisonment could quell Nelson Mandela's desire for the justice of others.

- **Todd Beamer, American software salesman and United Airlines Flight 93 passenger** – Recognizing the situation of the September 11, 2001 attack on his plane, he was one of the passengers who tried to reclaim the aircraft from the hijackers, leading them to crash it into a field in Stonycreek Township near Shanksville, Pennsylvania. Todd

Beamer's courageous actions in leading others and literally dying to self helped untold others live.

Living for others means putting ourselves last: our desires, our pride, our position.

But what if that's not easy for us?

More to the point: what if it isn't easy for me?

Sadly, I know a little bit about this. Well, actually, I know quite a bit about it: I'm one of them. Yet, God employed a drastic chain of events that, among several other aspects, would help shake me out of my selfishness:

- In 2004, my mother-in-law perished from stomach cancer that snatched her life at age 58.
- In 2005, my mom was diagnosed with thyroid cancer that would eventually, in 2014, claim her life at age 63.
- In 2008, as you know, my dad was diagnosed with frontotemporal dementia which in 2011 would quickly steal his life at age 63.
- In 2009, I lost my second sales job in five years, which nearly suffocated me through deep depression.
- In 2011, my dear bride, formerly so athletic and active, slipped and fell, instantly robbing her of her health. She would spend 14 months in bed. She suffers now from daily, often intense, pain and agony. Suzanne's health has been severely impacted.

Each of these circumstances led to a blaring crescendo that God used to rip me out of my selfish comfort zone and jolt me into the reality that He, indeed, wants me to serve others. God wants me to live for others.

Initially I became agitated, even lashing out at God, "How could you *do* this to *me*?!" Yep, it was all about me. Know anyone else like that? Yet God was so patient with me, even when my bride and others lost patience with me.

I'm by no means at the arrival point – never will be. But now, in retrospect, I consider it such a privilege to have been able to care for the people in my life whom I love the most: my family.

Here are some of the things God taught me along the way…

SO HOW DO I CARRY IT OUT?

- **Adjust our thinking** (Philippians 2:3) – Simple, huh?
  - Recognizing that my thinking is annoyingly self-centered, I received a rude awakening regarding the first aspect that I needed to change: my attitude. God desires us to view our daily walk with Him with excitement, not bitterness, and with joy, not drudgery.
  - Looking around at how God is walking with others is helpful, too. I began to look around me for others who were joyfully serving others, and I was embarrassed by how many people I saw happily serving despite their circumstances. My own self-reflection revealed something that abhorred me: I was falling far short of the mark.
  - Lastly, gather your courage and ask friends who have been longtime family servants to show you how, why, and what they do to serve others. You'll surely be encouraged, if not a little humbled, by what you learn. For example, I learned from a military buddy of mine how he cared for his wife, who suffered from Lupus, a degenerative disease similar to one of my own bride's ailments; the parallels are striking. It's easier to adjust your attitude when you realize your family isn't the only one going through a particular issue: you are not alone.
- **Pray for and with others** (1 Timothy 2:1) – Remember, praying is simply talking to God.

- Praying shifts our focus away from ourselves, centering instead on God and others. Praying for others is one of the most selfless acts we can perform. By praying for others, we transform from self-focused to others-focused; we arise as compassionate, available helpers.
- Most families are looking for you, Dad, to emerge as the spiritual leader of your household, and that can be a little intimidating. So keep it simple by taking the very doable step of initiating family prayer. Whether at meal or bed times, when something goes right, or something goes wrong, praying with your family not only sets a godly example for your family to follow, but tangibly places God in the center of your collective lives.
- And, remember, it's OK to pray for yourself. As the Yiddish saying goes, "Better to pray for yourself than to curse another." Even better, have your family "catch you" in the family room praying on your knees. The "What are you doing, Daddy?" questions will spark an amazing discussion, and help promote your lasting legacy in Christ.
- **Spend time with others** (1 Thessalonians 5:11) – Establish your relationships.
  - Plato wisely noted, "Be kind, for everyone you meet is fighting a harder battle." All of us are dealing with something, and spending time with others helps you intimately realize this. Specifically, by investing your time into your family, you will reap the dividends of not only better understanding them but also a more personal relationship.
  - Many times, we feel the world is aligned against us, that we're the only one going through junk. Yet, even as an "extroverted extrovert" as my bride calls me, the more time I spend with others, the more I realize that I've gotten wrapped up into my own cocoon, unable to fathom others' pain. Group time (e.g., dinners, vacations, and worship services) is super, but

don't forget to try to get one-on-one time with each of your family members. Perhaps the easiest way to do this is to join them in what they already like doing: playing sports; playing video games; spending time outdoors. Like my bride always encourages me: be available!

- Finally, spending time with another person challenges any preconceived notions I may hold about this person. God helps me more truly understand some of what this person is going through, what makes him or her go. A few of my kids are extroverts, though most are introverted; regardless, spending time with my kids better helps me understand them.

- **Engage in hospitality** (Hebrews 13:2) – Open your house – and your heart – to others.
    - The writer of Hebrews 13:2 (ESV) instructs, "Do not neglect to show hospitality to strangers, for thereby some have entertained angels unawares." We never know who exactly we're hosting; how exciting!
    - Some of our best memories and biggest belly laughs have come through hosting both extended family and long-lost friends. In one example, my bride and I were recently able to connect with a long-time mutual friend whom we were stationed with at Randolph Air Force Base in San Antonio, TX – we hadn't seen each other for 15 years. After his family was stationed at the United States Army War College in Carlisle, Pennsylvania, we've joined together on several joyous occasions bringing together a total 12 people under one roof.
    - My bride enjoys hosting our children's friends, so she can not only meet new people, but also have an opportunity to share Christ's love with them in a natural, disarming way. Suzanne frequently expresses that hospitality is one of her favorite undertakings.
- **Listen to others** (Proverbs 19:20) – That means me shutting my mouth and opening my ears.

- Wise King Solomon instructed in Proverbs 2:2 (NLT), "Tune your ears to wisdom and concentrate on understanding." By listening to others, we find it easier to live for others. As someone who enjoys talking, I find with my more quiet family members that I need to be comfortable with silence, and not worry about filling it in with my often constant conversation. Listening provides an opportunity to both savor our family time together as well as create an environment for more introverted family members to initiate conversation when and if it arises.
- Ernest Hemingway said, "I like to listen. I have learned a great deal from listening carefully. Most people never listen." Guilty as charged?
- On long car trips when I was in first grade, I would lean forward and ask my dad all kinds of crazy questions: How many broken yellow lines were painted on the road? How come there are so many billboards about food? Why are you driving so fast, Dad? Eventually Dad, not so subtlety masking his agitation, turned his head to me and almost pleaded, "Travis, why don't you sit back for a while and let your brother do the talking?" Why did Dad do that? Because he knew my brother had nothing to say! Ah, golden silence. Yet, that same golden silence helps us listen to others' true needs, their heart, and their desires.
- **Defer to others** (Luke 14:11) – This is the exact opposite of "It's my way...or the highway."
  - I shudder that Frank Sinatra so often still shouts out for me, "And more, much more than this, I did it my way." And that's the problem. When I make it all about me, I make others miserable. Here's the truth: **I'm most miserable when I'm thinking about myself.** Think on *that* one for a while....
  - When I consistently don't defer to others, I'm implicitly saying, "My way is better; you don't matter." Does it really

matter where I want to go to eat? What I want to talk about? What movie I want to see? Yes, there are times when we share our opinions and even the occasional need to stand up for ourselves, but, as I analyze my self-centered behavior, I too often refuse to defer to others because of my own comfort, my own stubbornness, my own way. An enormous area of growth for me has been deferring to my bride: what she wants to do, where she wants to go, what movie she'd like to catch, etc. Deferring to her is just one more way I can show her I love her in a way she'll not soon forget.

- Just as few seeds germinate on the path, few relationships grow when we consider only ourselves. Look for ways to lift others up over your own needs, to provide encouragement instead of always looking for it yourself. Jesus has plenty to share, so pass it along to others!

- **Celebrate with others** (Proverbs 11:2) – Be joyful for others.
  - We're not talking about birthday or New Year's parties or even Kool & the Gang's tune, "Celebrate good times, c'mon!", though parties are great fun. In view here: celebrating others' joys and accomplishments is key.
  - Regarding celebrating others' joys, I don't really know much about baseball, but when my men's small group wanted to catch a Saturday night ball game, I jumped at the chance. Yeah, I kind of understand baseball rules, but even though I don't favor the game, I delighted in seeing my buddies come alive in a new way. You can tell a lot about a man by how he lights up! It's the same with your family: celebrate their accomplishments, not in a patronizing way, but in a way that glorifies God working through us. For example, when my daughter earned a scholarship at a small, private Christian college, we praised God for His goodness, even as we celebrated our daughter's academic achievements. She truly

understands the gift God has given her, and how He allowed it to happen. Kudos, God!

- Regarding celebrating others' accomplishments, years ago I heard it said that if you can look upon someone else's work and be just as proud for them as you would be if it were your own work, you truly begin to understand what it means to celebrate with others. Some examples include: celebrating with your brother-in-law who just got the big promotion, even as you're still stalled at your own crummy job. Another: celebrating your dad's achievements, not feeling the need to "out-do" him. Always look for ways to think of yourself less and to think of others more (Luke 14:7-14). That makes Jesus proud. For example, try not to be like the high school educated father who insisted on building a bigger house than his college-educated children to compensate for his fears of underachievement. After all, we all can fall into a similar trap if we're not careful. So, don't compete, but celebrate with others!
- **The "Big 3"** – A brief review from Chapters 6 - 8.
  - Forgive others – While we covered this at some length in Chapter 6, it's worth reiterating that forgiving dad, among others, is a tremendous way to live for other people.
  - Reconcile with others – We considered this in Chapter 7, but it bears repeating that reconciliation with others is indeed a lifelong practice in how to live for others, especially your family.
  - Thank others – Lastly, while we stepped through this in Chapter 8, thanking your dad in a practical manner will grow your relationship with him.

As we close out this chapter let's review in Mark 9:37 (BSB) what Jesus said Himself about others, "Whoever welcomes one of these little children in

My name welcomes Me, and whoever welcomes Me welcomes not only Me, but the One who sent Me."

Jesus was specifically speaking about kids, but it's a basic reminder to welcome others, too.

Remember: Live out your faith and build your legacy by living for others.

CHALLENGE #10: Consider: What change(s) do you need to make to better live for others, especially your family? Start today!

CHAPTER 10 QUESTIONS:

1. So, who are the "OTHERS" God calls us to love?
2. In living for God, what's at least one practical way you can carry it out?
3. Consider **CHALLENGE #10**: What change(s) do you need to make to better live for others, especially your family?

11

JESUS DEMONSTRATES HIS LASTING LEGACY

"Now that you know these things you will be blessed if you do them."

JOHN 13:17 (NIV)

"The merit of all things lies in their difficulty."

~ *ANDREW DUMAS*, THE THREE MUSKETEERS

JESUS DEMONSTRATES HIS lasting legacy through one of the Bible's most vulnerable stories: Jesus washes His disciples' feet (John 13:1-17). This is perhaps the most intimate moment of Jesus' teaching, surpassed only by His forthcoming work on the cross just one day later.

The site of His vulnerable service is, of course, the Upper Room (Luke 22:12). Jesus called His disciples here to prepare them to celebrate the Passover together on Thursday evening of Passion Week. Recognizing the urgency of

His situation (Matthew 26:29), Jesus offers a compelling personal testimony of how we are to love and serve Him and others.

For the past three years, Jesus' earthly ministry had consisted of walking the Holy Land, teaching the masses, healing the sick, and praising God both publicly and privately. He was always teaching, always reinforcing, always glorifying God. Yet, by at least one measure, His teaching of late seemed not to have "stuck" very well based on at least two accounts:

- Luke reveals in 9:46 (NLT), "Then his disciples began arguing about which of them was the greatest." >>Wince<< Scripture does not say whether He was annoyed or not, but Jesus patiently taught through His own disciples' selfishness.
- In the account of A Mother's Request (Matthew 20:20-28 ISV), the mother of James and John, two of the three disciples in Jesus' "inner circle" (Peter as well), asked Jesus, "Promise that in Your kingdom these two sons of mine will sit on Your right and on Your left" (Matthew 28:24). In other words, "Can my two darling sons be raised to prominence over the other disciples?" Of course, the other disciples were agitated by her boldness.

At this point, I wonder if Jesus might have been thinking, "After three years of sitting under my teaching and this is their attitude towards servanthood?!" So, Jesus took a common foot washing ritual, a menial task often performed by slaves, to demonstrate an eternal lesson of selfless service to others. And Jesus' act here is among His finest examples of just Who He is.

Explains Burge, "Foot washing was a common custom due to the wearing of sandals and the dry, dusty Palestinian roads. A good host would provide a servant who would work in this capacity, but if none were there he certainly would not take up the chore himself as Jesus does (13:4-5). That which enables Jesus to serve like this may be described in John 13:3. Jesus has perfect self-esteem: he knows of God's love expressed in his origin and destiny, and therefore can relinquish human status to become a servant."

Jesus Washes His Disciples' Feet (John 13:1-17 NIV)

[1]It was just before the Passover Feast. Jesus knew that the time had come for him to leave this world and go to the Father. Having loved his own who were in the world, he now showed them the full extent of his love.

[2]The evening meal was being served, and the devil had already prompted Judas Iscariot, son of Simon, to betray Jesus. [3]Jesus knew that the Father had put all things under his power, and that he had come from God and was returning to God; [4]so he got up from the meal, took off his outer clothing, and wrapped a towel around his waist. [5]After that, he poured water into a basin and began to wash his disciples' feet, drying them with the towel that was wrapped around him.

[6]He came to Simon Peter, who said to him, "Lord, are you going to wash my feet?"

[7]Jesus replied, "You do not realize now what I am doing, but later you will understand."

[8]"No," said Peter, "you shall never wash my feet."

Jesus answered, "Unless I wash you, you have no part with me."

[9]"Then, Lord," Simon Peter replied, "not just my feet but my hands and my head as well!"

[10]Jesus answered, "A person who has had a bath needs only to wash his feet; his whole body is clean. And you are clean, though not every one of you." [11]For he knew who was going to betray him, and that was why he said not every one was clean.

[12]When he had finished washing their feet, he put on his clothes and returned to his place. "Do you understand what I have done for you?" he asked them. [13]"You call me 'Teacher' and 'Lord,' and rightly so, for that is what I am. [14]Now that I, your Lord and Teacher, have washed your feet, you also should wash one another's feet. [15]I have set you an example that you should do as I have done for you. [16]I tell you the truth, no servant is greater than his master, nor is a messenger greater than the one who sent him.

[17]Now that you know these things, you will be blessed if you do them. John 13:1-17 (NIV)

LESSON FROM JESUS WASHES HIS DISCIPLES' FEET

- **Time is short** (John 13:1) – Jesus sensed the urgency, since not only was His own earthly ministry ending, but also His time with His disciples. I would realize much later that my own dad's imminent passing was a lesson of similar urgency.
- **Satan thinks he has a play** (John 13:2) – Then, like now, Satan still tries to muck things up.
- **Jesus serves** (John 13:3-5) – Jesus wanted to teach His disciples a simple, tangible but lasting lesson on what it means to serve.
- **Jesus will surprise you** (John 13:6-7) – Jesus' mode of service surprised even His disciples.
- **An uncomfortable truth** (John 13:8) – Sacrificial service is essential for Christ followers.
- **The moment of understanding** (John 13:12-14) – Even though Christ is "teacher" and "Lord" He served others; He didn't have an "out" clause for degrading tasks.
- **The supreme example** (John 13:15-16) – In serving others, Jesus offers us a supreme example that He desires us to replicate.
- **The practical lesson** (John 13:17) – "Now that you know these things, you will be blessed if you do them."

But the **prime lesson**, the overarching theme of Jesus washing His disciples' feet, is how Jesus so tangibly demonstrated His own supreme commitment to living for God, who ordered Him to the cross, and to living for others, by dying for us on the cross! Jesus provided the ultimate legacy of service: washing their feet was simply a prelude to history's grandest, humblest act of servitude: taking on the sin of man for our redemption. Jesus knew the vast majority of us would never be crucified or even martyred, so He gave His disciples and, in turn, us, a simple example of how to leave a lasting legacy – His legacy – by sacrificial service.

Let me confess now: one particular element of this story makes me uncomfortable, *extremely* uncomfortable. It's not that I'm uncomfortable with Jesus serving in such a vulnerable and demeaning way. It's just that the "washing feet" thing totally creeps me out. Now, I know many Anglican, Lutheran, Methodist, and other denominations participate in Holy Week foot-washing ceremonies, so I mean no disrespect at all. It's just something that gives me the heebie-jeebies. In my youth, my brother and I served as church janitors, washing toilets and urinals barehanded with toothbrushes and toilet brushes – none of that ever bothered me. Nails on a chalkboard – child's play by comparison. Yet, for some reason, Jesus washing His disciples' feet – the dirty feet part – really makes me squirm. Now that I've driven my quirk into the ground, you'll see how this all relates to the narrative as I turn now to my dear, dying dad, Gary "Smoke" Zimmerman.

CHALLENGE #11: How does Jesus' supreme example of living for God and others impact your view of your own lasting legacy?

CHAPTER 11 QUESTIONS:

1. Why was Jesus washing His disciples' feet so shocking to the Apostle Peter?
2. What would you say is a main lesson of Jesus Washes His Disciples' Feet (John 13:1-17)?
3. Consider **CHALLENGE #11:** How does Jesus' supreme example of living for God and others impact your view of your own lasting legacy?

12

LEGACY CARRIED ON IN MY LIFE'S MOST VULNERABLE MOMENT

"They will be called oaks of righteousness, a planting of the LORD for the display of His splendor."

ISAIAH 61:3 (NIV)

"Smoke's legacy will be the values that we take with us and impart to our children."

~ LONGTIME FRIEND OF THE FAMILY

GUT-WRENCHING. AWKWARD. LIFE-THREATENING.

Do I have your attention?

We've discussed living for God and others, and the practical ways we can leave a lasting legacy: by leading our families as we follow Christ. And we've already seen that being a faithful dad requires personal commitment, but it also requires an awareness that looks beyond the surface and outside of ourselves. Now it really gets personal.

You see, we're often all too aware of the sometimes forgettable legacy we perceive we're leaving that we miss the moments when we actually *are* leaving a lasting legacy. And – all drama aside – my life's most vulnerable moment left me so out of sorts that at the time I didn't realize what God was doing.

GARY "SMOKE" ZIMMERMAN

Gary "Smoke" Zimmerman, circa 2004

Through this guide I've shared several stories about my dad, so I'll only share a few more details now as they relate to my most vulnerable moment I'm about to share. My dad was a "man's man", a forester by trade for nearly 40 years and, like most foresters, he was a man of few words. Trees have little to say! And, while most people identify trees by their leaves (think of your 9th grade biology leaf project!), not my dad. Dad not only knew trees by their bark and their Latin name, but also by their *taste*. At a forestry school outdoor lab, legend has it that Dad, spying an unidentified vine, snapped off a young twig and popped it into his mouth to identify the vine. The entire forestry class watched in horror, eyes as wide as unexplored caves, as Dad offered his analysis: poison ivy! Of course, Dad didn't get poison ivy, something many other foresters envied in Dad.

Dad stood 6' tall, but his barrel-chest, his deep voice, his trademark handlebar mustache and his ability to fix most anything contributed to the aura of respect my dad commanded both far and wide. Though we didn't grow up on a farm per se, we did raise laying chickens. One day, when Dad noticed one of our hens had stopped laying brown eggs, he investigated and discovered that she had been eating hay. To Dad, this presented a production problem. So, rather than put the chicken down, Dad elected to perform surgery. With the patience of a country veterinarian, Dad carefully secured the hen and employed a sharp Exacto knife to carefully execute a longitudinal cut down the sickly hen's throat. Through the incision, Dad skillfully dislodged the straw and then proceeded to close up the incision by sewing it shut with fishing line. Who knew? Soon after, the once ailing hen began laying brown eggs again – production problem solved!

Yet, as passionate as Dad was about his work, his hobbies, and his life, nothing eclipsed his passion for his family. He saw it as his overarching duty to take care of his bride and take care of his family. So you can easily imagine how devastating it was for both him and us when Dad gradually began to get sick: the head of the house, the rock we relied on, was losing his memory. Something was *very* wrong.

Dad has always been a stickler for details with a cop-like instinct for the subtleties of any given situation. But he shocked us over the span of several months when he forgot to renew his vehicle registration, struggled to balance his checkbook, and grappled with using his computer, among other issues. In June 2008 as spring transitioned into summer, Mom approached me privately asking, "Have you noticed your dad acting strangely?" We compared notes and emerged even more alarmed by the frightening pattern we saw in Dad's behavior. More troublesome, my formerly even-keeled, emotionally stolid dad increasingly engaged in overly passionate rants, often breaking down in tears as he moaned that he couldn't understand what was happening to his mind.

Just days after Mom and I compared notes, Dad completed a critical follow-up appointment with a noted neurologist. The doctor pronounced a horrific death sentence: at age 60, Dad was diagnosed with frontotemporal dementia (FTD). In short, Dad's brain was dying, so Dad was dying. Here are three ways to describe Dad's death sentence:

- **Clinically:** FTD is a group of related conditions resulting from the progressive degeneration of the temporal and frontal lobes of the brain. These areas of the brain play a significant role in decision-making, behavioral control, emotion and language.
- **Layman's terms:** Your frontal lobe is the center of your emotions and personality – it's what makes you, you. FTD is like a hairdryer blast that gradually, fatally shrinks your frontal lobe. In fact, as my dad's disease progressed, his head became visibly disfigured as his temples drastically sunk in to fill the space vacated by his diseased brain.
- **The Reality:** Watching Dad's deathly decline was like watching a stick of butter melting in a hot skittle.

I have never cried more in my entire life: watching Dad, my hero, fade and slip away from us. As both time and Dad's disease progressed, Dad grew increasingly suicidal, inconsolable, and uncontrollable. Because we were less and less able to negotiate Dad's outbreaks, Mom assented to temporarily placing Dad in the local hospital's psychiatric unit: the very place God would stage my life's most vulnerable moment.

SUNDAY, JUNE 28, 2009

By the time Dad was admitted in the psych unit, he was a shrunken shadow of the broad-shouldered, loving family man he had been before. During the admission process, he made an immediate dash for the exit door. It took six strong people to restrain him, so powerfully determined was Dad to resist. Only after a shot of morphine did Dad begin to calm down. To me, I saw little difference between my Dad's situation and a tranquilized safari animal. Frontotemporal dementia was certainly living up to all that it "promised" to be – devastating to both the afflicted and the family.

From the day Dad was admitted, we were only permitted to see him briefly during visiting hours. Mom and I jumped at the opportunity to check in on Dad. We discovered he was visibly agitated by his predicament. Only after considerable prodding would Dad concede to walk the halls with us. On my first and only visit to the psych unit, Mom took Dad's right hand, and I his left, and the three of us walked the hallways in a sweeping, methodical oval. Just as our pattern remained the same, so were Dad's attempts to escape. Each time Dad encountered a locked exit door on our walk, he would bull rush it, dragging Mom and me along like spineless ragdolls as he simultaneously slammed into the door, bellowing, "LET ME OUT OF HERE!" After several laps and escape attempts, I could sense Mom's exhaustion, and, totally unnerved by Dad's present condition, I secretly searched for a way out of this frighteningly surreal environment. I attempted to plan my escape, but God had other plans He was soon to reveal. The odors wafting off my father presently brought me back.

You see, it was immediately evident upon approaching Dad that he hadn't shaved or showered in days. I remember thinking: this is not my problem, someone else will take care of Dad's hygiene. And now that we had completed Dad's walk, it seemed a natural breakoff point to end this living nightmare. As Mom and Dad continued down the hall without me, I thought I'd make use of Dad's bathroom before hitting the road, but what I discovered next stopped me cold. There, in Dad's private bathroom I found that the shower stall floor was a repository for all sorts of towels and washcloths, all of them thoroughly soaked.

Confusion struck me: Did Dad really need a shower, since it appeared he had already taken one? Why else would there be wet towels on the floor of the shower? As I reflected on this riddle, I individually wrung out each of the sopping wet towels and washcloths and hung them up to dry.

Rejoining Dad and Mom as they looped towards me, I still pondered the shower mystery, when she asked me an audacious question, "Travis, it's been quite a while since Dad has shaved. Would you be willing to shave him?"

My mind raced, my mouth clamped shut as my eyes searched out the nearest EXIT sign, and my will was put to the test as I silently screamed: ARE YOU KIDDING ME? You want me to hold a razor to the neck of a crazy, dying man? That's suicide – my dad's going to rip me apart! I'm going to tell her, No, this is completely unreasonable, Mom; nobody in the history of the world has done this. OK, now it's my turn to tell Mom just what I think: NO WAY, NO HOW, NO, NO, NO!

Instead, almost as if having an out-of-body experience, I heard my lips exclaim, "Sure, Mom, I'm glad to help Dad."

There's a first time for everything: today was my day to shave my dad. Awkward.

I slowly extended my hand and gently grasped Dad's calloused hand – Dad's hand still swallowed mine – and led him towards the bathroom; he trailed behind me like a lost sheep. There, drawing tepid water for the job, I swished a white washcloth around the gathering fluid. The more I swirled my hands around in the water, the more easily I was able set my questioning mind at ease. Dad jarred me back to full consciousness as he huskily cleared his throat. Was he on to me? Was Dad preparing to turn the tables on me again like he had done so many times before in his illness? Snapping to, I abruptly lifted the washcloth from the sink, slowly wrung the excess water out, and applied a warm compress to Dad's stiff whiskered face to soften it up. Though Dad was oblivious to it, tears welled up in my eyes as I recalled Dad teaching me how to shave at age 15. Now, it was me who was shaving Dad. The bitter intimacy of it all was almost too much to bear. As I held Dad's head in both of my hands, a "too close for comfort" invasion of his personal space, it seemed to me as if I were holding the head of a dragon. It's not that my dad was ever a monster, but, as the looming authoritarian figure of our house, he didn't invite this kind of physical closeness, even in his illness. I had *never* been in a position to be this physically close to him. Even though it took six medical workers to restrain him, I found I still feared...and revered him.

Clumsily I spread an uneven gelatinous pile of shaving cream around his face, doing my best to level it out. It was similar to trying to teach your young son how to tie his necktie – easier done on yourself than on another. Exhaling my now pent up breath and sensing my own heart thumping out of my chest, I gently scraped the slowly-crystalizing shaving cream off his face with a disposable razor – a far cry from the manly double-edged razor Dad used, and, in turn, started Eric and me off with. I trembled that Dad would grab my neck, snapping it like a brittle pine twig. But Mom had asked me to perform my duty, in the same manner Dad taught me: a man always does his duty.

As I finished up this less-than-perfect shave my thoughts again returned to pulling off my own jailbreak, pronto. No sooner had the thought entered my mind when Dad mumbled, "I gotta take a leak." No matter: Dad's private bathroom boasted both a commode and a shower. Dad turned towards the commode, but instead of stopping there to relieve himself, he lumbered to his right, stopping in front of the open shower stall. And, there, Dad urinated onto the shower floor.

Suddenly it dawned on me: Dad hadn't had a shower after all. All those soaked towels and washcloths I had hung up were, well, drenched in a manner I hadn't anticipated. I felt terrible for Dad again, but took this moment to wash my hands really, really, really well. I remember nervously chuckling to myself: it almost broke the pervasive tension. Good one, Dad!

OK, this was enough: first the shave, now the urine-soaked towels. I started the short distance from Dad's bathroom to the nearest exit, but Mom, sensing I was slipping away, doubled down on the audacious question. I didn't know it then, but her question would change my life forever. "Travis, thank you for shaving Dad. But it's also been about a week since he's showered. Would you mind giving your dad a shower?"

Are you KIDDING ME, Mom?! That's against Dad's "Man Rules": you gotta spit six feet to be a man; you always open car doors for your mom…and wasn't showering alone with your dad somewhere in there? There's no WAY Dad, in his right mind, would ever concede to this! There's no way, never, ever, ever. I would just have to stick to my guns and tell her that I'm not doing it. Selfishness gripped me.

Yet, my mouth betrayed me as I obediently answered Mom's question. "Sure, Mom," I lied, "I'm happy to help…."

By this time, Dad had shuffled from the shower stall and was standing by himself. I hadn't noticed it before, but Dad's appearance rudely stunned me, although I wasn't able to immediately identify why that was. Dad was still "Dad" but bereft of clothes and absent in his gaze. Then it hit me: Dad just *looked* sick, particularly in his posture. He stood aright, but his torso was bent to the right, crooked like the trees Dad himself would have methodically straightened with bamboo stakes so many times in his forestry career. Yet, Dad was beyond straightening, beyond my persistent prayer that God would heal my dad on earth. I knew this in my heart, and it made we want to approach the shower stall, not to urinate, but to vomit. Still shoving my emotions aside, I forced my glaring frown into a grim look of determination as I prayed for God's help and then started Dad's shower.

This was going to be a challenge. First, because it's a psych ward, the shower head was fixed to the shower wall: no energizing massage, no wide spray, just a plain, fixed metal shower head like you might have found in any prison. Pun intended. Second, this shower had no shower curtain nor a shower rod for patient safety reasons. Third – and this is the big one – this wasn't your standard tub shower with plenty of room for baths or standing or singing in the shower. No, this was a STALL shower, hardly bigger than a telephone booth. Both are intended for *exactly ONE* man at a time.

I glanced back at Dad and was unnerved. This man, who rarely kept still, even more so as his brain became increasingly disease-ravaged, hadn't moved an inch. His stance cemented as he lurched to the side, staring somewhere into the distance, somewhere not here. The silent bathroom reminded me of a makeshift morgue: cool, antiseptic, lonely.

Returning my attention to the shower, I absently fumbled with the shower controls to dial up some warm water for Dad. Why was it taking so long? With the glacier speed of a decades-old plumbing system, warm water eventually found its way to the showerhead, and the tepid moisture stream signaled my hand that it was time to wash my dad.

"Your shower's ready, Dad," I mechanically announced as if pronouncing a sentence for a sixth grade spelling bee. Dad's head swiveled to meet my eyes and, in a glance, I knew he understood.

Dad trudged slowly into the shower. Despite the warm water on this blazing summer's day, a chill flashed down my spine as Dad settled alone in the shower-for-one. You see, rather than preparing himself for a shower like you or I might do, Dad instead walked into the shower, stopping when he could go no further. It was as if he was at a dead end and he couldn't even turn himself around to face me. Caught in a maze, Dad was like a rat who had just surrendered to his fate. Most disturbingly, Dad stood in the exact same crooked stance as before, leaning to the side, apparently oblivious to the water running down his back. My tears began again, burning my cheeks as I silently mumbled these words to myself, "Oh, Lord, Dad looks so sick; Dad is so sick."

Caught up once more in my own emotions, I gradually became aware that I was getting wet from the shower water deflecting off my dad onto my street clothes. Annoyed that my initial "wash Dad quickly and dryly" strategy wasn't working, and that I was getting drenched, I subconsciously took a step or two backward to keep dry. In retrospect, the symbolism here was obvious: I don't want to get involved here, it's too wet, too uncomfortable.

Yet, I had a job to do, a job I had promised to accomplish for Mom. Inhaling slowly, then quickly exhaling, I devised a plan to stay dry: I removed my sandals. Big step! Due to the physical distance I had placed between us, I realized that if I bent forward, really, really bent forward, I could *just* wash my dad's back and not get wet. An outside observer checking in on this curious method would have noted something strange: my body was contorted into the shape of a "C" with my hands and feet closest to my dad, and my rear end pointed away from him. Of course, my own contorted stance felt completely unnatural, looked absolutely ridiculous, and I had a growing fear that Mom would arrive unannounced only to be incensed at her older son's squeamishness. Yet, the fear of Mom catching me didn't dissuade my own stay-dry shower-washing posture: I continued to *try* to wash Dad, but I was getting nowhere. It was then I sensed the Holy Spirit whisper to me, "Travis, wash your father."

Now, I'm not the world's most perceptive guy, so God has been very patient with me as He's teaching me. Most of the time, I hear from God when I'm reading His Word: He speaks so clearly and sweetly through the ages and pages of His Word. Yet, I've learned He will occasionally whisper to me through His Spirit and, from my experience, what He's telling me is usually something I *don't* want to hear. No, I won't hear commands like, "Travis, you need to move to Orlando... (echoing: Orlando, Orlando)."

No, I'll usually hear something I don't want to do like, "Travis, the words you used when referring to the opposing soccer coach don't bring glory and honor to Me: apologize to the coach and then apologize to your team." Ouch! I'm not saying the Holy Spirit never says anything "positive" to me, but when I sensed Him nudging me, "Travis, wash your father," I knew I was in His crosshairs.

And Dad stood there in the shower, crooked as a wind-weathered oak, as the water slipped over his body, running down the drain at his feet.

It was time to amp up my game. I decided now to also remove my shirt and shorts: *this* will prevent me from getting my clothes wet. Shamefully, I assumed the exact same "C" position myself, trying to wash Dad and *not* get wet, looking even more ridiculous now than before: a grown man in his underwear trying – but miserably failing – to wash his dying father. A poisonous thought settled into my head, one that I still cannot shake. I'm ashamed to even share it here, but the Holy Spirit would have it no other way. I had removed all my clothes except my underwear, and contorted myself into this "C" shower-washing posture, because I didn't want to get wet as I washed Dad. But, in my heart of hearts, it wasn't so much that I didn't want to get wet: I became aware that I didn't want to be this closely associated with this dying husk of a man who was now my dad. It's a regretful reality of life that it's easy to hang out with family and friends who are "normal" and living life to the fullest, but if you get sick, people ditch you. I was in danger of doing just that to my own dad, my greatest mentor, my hero.

And Dad stood there in the shower, crooked as a wind-weathered oak, as the water slipped over his body, running down the drain at his feet.

The Holy Spirit thankfully intervened again in a most uncomfortable, but strangely welcome way, "Travis, get into the shower with your dad." I was busted. I distinctly remember protruding my head upward, crying out aloud to Him, "Oh, God, please give me strength to do this. PLEASE!" My lips pursed into a contrived, toothless smile as my gaze returned to the floor; Dad remained motionless like the seasoned deer hunter he was of old, yet now he was unaware of his surroundings.

So, dropping the remaining vestiges of both my pride and my solo article of clothing, I finally understood what God was asking me to do: to stop pretending to wash my dad and do the job right.

Casting a humiliated glance upward to God, I approached the one-person stall shower, filled with my dad's still imposing frame. I cautiously contorted my body not into a "C" posture as before, but into an equally uncomfortable one: I positioned myself behind my father, facing his back, water spraying all over me, temporarily blinding my eyes. And, while to Dad it was a memory surrendered to disease, I was again absolutely certain I was in clear violation of one of Dad's "Man Rules": "Stall showers are for one man only." After trying so much and fighting so hard to avoid it, here I was at last: father and son, in a one-man stall shower. We were both naked, and, for once, I felt no shame.

I was very *un*comfortable. No room to move, no excuse should Mom show up now unannounced. It was time to get to work, to do what both Mom asked me to do, what God told me to do, and what I needed to do: wash Dad.

I seized the flimsy soap bar, and, finding I had left the washcloth at the sink after Dad's shave, I improvised: with my right hand, I furiously circled the soap into a frenzied lather in my left hand. Remembering Dad's degraded condition and the fact that he couldn't see me, I spoke softly into his left ear, "Dad, I'm going to wash your head now." And, sensing no resistance, I scrubbed the top of his bald head, gently cleaned his face as best I could, and then his neck. Time to reload.

I continued to explain what I was going to do. "Dad, I'm going to wash your back now." Again, no apparent comprehension. It was getting even more uncomfortable now as I tried to create some space to wash his back. Cramped as we were and realizing Dad wasn't moving, I jammed my own back against the shower wall, producing just enough clearance to soap up his back. This, time, however I made it all the way down to his calves before reloading.

Returning to standing position as I worked the rapidly diminishing soap bar into one last sudsy heap, I reflected how vulnerable, defenseless, and lost my Dad was as his mind was shutting down. It was like a janitor shutting down the dozens of rows of lights in a gymnasium, one breaker at a time: CLICK-CLICK-CLICK. Here was Dad, my prime role model, and the man who loomed largest in my life, dying right in front of me. I think I was so traumatized by Dad's vulnerable state that I didn't even know how to react. Yet even as washed him, I realized that God was imprinting a memory in indelible ink, a lifelong memory of my last days with my dad. I also realized then, honestly, that I was no different than my dad. We had the same mannerisms, the same booming voice, the same competitive spirit, the same devotion to our wife and kids, and the same Lord. And then it hit me: someday someone might be washing me in the same way. I prayed to God for Him to deliver Dad home and heal him.

"Dad," I announced through my stinging tears and shaky voice, "I'm going to wash your feet now." And, just like that, God worked through me to finish the job in my life's most vulnerable moment. I returned to an upright position and did the only thing left to do: I held my dying dad there in the shower, a hug I will never, ever forget.

And Dad and I stood there in the shower, crooked as wind-weathered oaks, as the water and my bitter tears slipped over our bodies, running down the drain at our feet.

As I later recounted this tender story to a good friend, he pointed out that, in washing Dad's body, I had washed Dad's feet, just as Jesus commanded…I hadn't even grasped it.

¹²When he had finished washing their feet, he put on his clothes and returned to his place. "Do you understand what I have done for you?" he asked them. ¹³"You call me 'Teacher' and 'Lord,' and rightly so, for that is what I am. ¹⁴Now that I, your Lord and Teacher, have washed your feet, you also should wash one another's feet. ¹⁵I have set you an example that you should do as I have done for you. ¹⁶I tell you the truth, no servant is greater than his master, nor is a messenger greater than the one who sent him. ¹⁷Now that you know these things, you will be blessed if you do them. John 13:12-17 (NIV)

I close now with the lessons God taught me through my life's most vulnerable moment:

- **Dad couldn't, but I could:** You know why God told me to wash Dad's feet (and his body)? Because Dad wasn't able to do it himself! God will frequently ask us to help others who can't help themselves.

- **I wouldn't, but Jesus could** – Jesus helped me in my shame to serve dad. This wasn't a disassociated help, but an "I'll walk with you" to wash Dad. Jesus would show this same type of love in going to the cross for our sins. We wouldn't, be He could and did.

- **Get out of your own way:** God knew that my initial selfishness and pride were preventing me from acting in my dad's best interest. Get over yourself and get out of the way.

- **The perfect role model:** Jesus modeled His legacy in John 13:17, "Now that you know these things, you will be blessed if you do them." This is a key aspect of God's lasting legacy to us!

- **A faithful dad:** Dad modeled his own legacy by the real, honorable, honest life he tried to live in supporting his family. This was my dad's lasting legacy to me!

- **Follow suit:** By following our Faithful Father's perfect legacy who inspired my own faithful dad's human legacy. Through the Holy Spirit we will be able to leave our own legacy that glorifies God!

- **Blind spot:** Like my mom did for me, it may require others to help you see your duty.

- **An unrealized legacy:** Sometimes we think we're leaving a forgettable legacy with little impact until someone points it out to us - I had washed my father's feet and hadn't even realized it! In doing so, God used that to create part of my own legacy, an unrealized legacy.
- **Serve in strength?** It's wonderful to serve in our areas of strength, but sometimes God calls us to serve Him and others in the most vulnerable of situations. "My grace is sufficient for you, for My power is made perfect in weakness." 2 Corinthians 12:9 (NIV)
- **Serve in weakness!** You may never be called to wash your dad's feet, but God will call you to something similar: <u>don't lean away from it, lean *into* it!</u>

Dad continued to lose motor function, spending his last months in a forlorn dementia unit, endlessly walking the halls day and night as any forester might walk his woods. Yet not a day passed in those 15 months that Mom did not faithfully visit her beloved but fading husband.

My final encounter with my dad occurred just days before he passed. As I lethargically punched in the access code to gain entry to the dementia unit, I spotted Dad shuffling towards me at a slow, mechanical pace, almost as if he were unable to bend his knees. It had been months since he recognized me, but to my surprise, Dad, spotting my eyes, jutted out his right hand for me to shake as he approached me. Grabbing firm hold of it and looking him in the eye, just as he had taught me as a young boy, I shook it vigorously, then closed the distance between us with a bear hug. But even before completing our hug, a nurse approached Dad from behind, pulling his pants out to check on his diaper. "You need a diaper change, Smoke." With that, she jammed a shot of morphine into Dad's neck and hustled him off to change his soiled diaper. I never saw him alive again.

Hours later, as Dad wandered his own trail of sorrows, he finally collapsed from years of diseased decay and exhaustion, falling backward and cracking his skull open, not unlike the brown chicken eggs he once looked after;

he never regained consciousness. And God answers prayer, so faithfully, so mercifully: on May 13, 2011 at 10 p.m., Jesus took Dad home; Mom relayed the bitter news by phone. Yet, as we would later piece together, at the exact moment of Dad's passing, the Holy Spirit awoke my son, Grant, from his nightmare. Through a rush of tears, Grant wailed his own announcement, "Dad-Dad is gone! Dad-Dad is gone!" Smoke Zimmerman's suffering saw its end in God's eternal glory.

Weeks later, our beloved former pastor remembered Dad at his celebration of life service by sharing the Scripture verse, Isaiah 61:3 (NIV). He chose it because it most reminded him of Smoke Zimmerman, "They will be called oaks of righteousness, a planting of the LORD for the display of His splendor." From my vantage point in the raised pulpit, I was humbled to see dozens of mourners softly, tearfully nodding in agreement.

And Dad, my faithful dad, once crooked as a wind-weathered oak, is now a planting of the LORD for the display of His splendor. He is healed forever, his lasting legacy secured in Christ.

Follow my example, as I follow the example of Christ. 1 Corinthians 11:1 (NIV)

CHALLENGE #12: What vulnerable act of service is God calling you to perform? Now, serve outside of your comfort zone.

CHAPTER 12 QUESTIONS:

1. Why is it sometimes so difficult for us to understand what God has called us to do?
2. When it comes to serving in hard times, how do you interpret the saying, "don't lean away from it, lean *into* it?"

3. Consider **CHALLENGE #12**: What vulnerable act of service is God call you to perform? Now, serve outside of your comfort zone.

Gary "Smoke" Zimmerman's family at the dedication of the "Smoke" Zimmerman Cross-Country Ski Trail in the Michaux State Forest where he worked near Fayetteville, Pennsylvania. Clearly, my faithful dad left a legacy firmly secured in Christ!

PART 4

REVIEW AND CONCLUSION

13

REVIEW

Follow my example, as I follow the example of Christ.

1 CORINTHIANS 11:1 (NIV)

"Anyone can be a father, but it takes someone special to be a dad, and that's why I call you dad, because you are so special to me. You taught me the game and you taught me how to play it right."

~WADE BOGGS

OK, FAITHFUL DADS, we've been encouraged, humbled, lifted up, and shown Christ's perfect example of living for God and living for others. Now it's time to review what we've learned and carry it forward.

PART 1 LAYING THE FOUNDATION

CHAPTER 1 A LASTING LEGACY

We first sought to understand the term *legacy* by drawing on Merriam-Webster's definition as, "something transmitted by or received from an ancestor or predecessor." In layman's terms this is how people both in this generation and the next perceive our memory. We noted that many legacies are characterized by names left behind on inanimate objects such as the Washington Memorial but were quickly sobered by how those legacies faded like the crumbling Parthenon of ancient times past. More personally, we recognized the folly in making our legacy about us. It was here we introduced this guide's central idea: **a legacy – a lasting legacy – is about you, Dad, wholeheartedly following Jesus and leading your family to do the same.**

CHAPTER 2 LEGACY: THE QUESTION V. THE REALITY

This naturally led us to arguably one of the most, if not *the* most, critical question a dad will ever answer.

The Question: What legacy do I want to leave for my family?

As we talked through this question we were reminded of the finite time we each have on Earth, and a somewhat uncomfortable reality emerged.

The Reality: Whether you know it or not, you're already leaving a legacy. But what legacy?

CHAPTER 3 FOLLOW MY EXAMPLE, AS I FOLLOW THE EXAMPLE OF CHRIST

This reality prompted no small amount of soul-searching and led us to the perfect example of legacy embodied in this guide's key Scripture.

Key Verse: Follow my example, as I follow the example of Christ. 1 Corinthians 11:1 (NIV)

You'll recall this was the Apostle Paul's challenge to the churches he established, so his followers would not simply follow him alone, but ultimately follow Jesus. We devoted some time discussing the often elusive task of being able to strike the right balance between modelling our own example and modelling Christ. It was here I shared the awkward example of a dog lying vulnerably on his back and referenced 2 Corinthians 12:9 (NIV), "My grace is sufficient for you, for My power is made perfect in weakness." We agreed that to leave a lasting legacy for your family, keep Jesus in the center of your life and let Him work through your discomfort. Our ways, our words, and our world will perish, but Jesus stands forever. We leave a lasting legacy, not when we build upon the crust of the earth, but when we build upon the cross of Christ! And it was here that we committed 1 Corinthians 11:1 to memory.

CHAPTER 4 A FAITHFUL DAD: WHO IS HE?

With our central theme, big question, reality, and key verse established, the final piece of laying the foundation involved actually defining a faithful dad: Who is he? We found overwhelming biblical definitions of faith. Further, I opined that being a dad is God's highest privilege to men. Being a dad encompasses so much of what God has created us to be. In fact, the prerequisite for being a faithful dad is first of all being a man of God. We also highlighted the distinction between a father and a dad, and the difference in the level of relationship being a dad is. Yet God never called us to be dads all by ourselves, and we realized the futility of going it alone: we need God to be a faithful dad! A life-changing insight we uncovered together is that God is *The* Faithful Dad, our model to be a faithful dad. Recall that our kids will follow us most anywhere, even up the face of an active volcano! No wonder it's so important to follow Jesus as we lead our family.

PART 2 LEGACY: THE PAST IS PROLOGUE

CHAPTER 5 BUT YOU DON'T KNOW MY DAD...

From here we transitioned to the guide's second main part which asserts that with our legacy, the past is prologue. That is, so often events in our past drive the way we move forward. Though some of us had fantastic dads and others had uneventful childhoods, many of us suffered from dads ranging from uninvolved to uninspired to dysfunctional to abusive. Don't worry: you're not alone. Each of us either prayed that God would soften our heart towards our dad or we prayed in thankfulness for our own faithful dad. It was here that we laid out a three-step process that mirrors Jesus' own earthly walk: I forgive you, Dad (because Jesus forgives); Peace, Dad (because Jesus reconciled with us); and Thank you, Dad (because Jesus encourages thankfulness).

CHAPTER 6 I FORGIVE YOU, DAD (BECAUSE JESUS FORGIVES)

In the first stage of this process, we examined forgiveness, noting the wisdom of the anonymously shared saying, "Not forgiving someone is like drinking poison and expecting the other person to die." We defined forgiveness as the act of ending anger against someone. We then took a closer look at some of the main reasons we often choose to hang onto unforgiveness, several of them embarrassing and painful, but, frankly, none of them justified. Remember: forgiveness is always a choice. Through Jesus's Parable of the Unmerciful Servant (Matthew 18:21-35) we can sum up His primary lesson here: God has forgiven us, so He expects us to forgive others. So, if there is a need, forgive your dad, remembering God forgives our sins. Follow my example, as I follow the example of Christ... by forgiving your dad.

CHAPTER 7 PEACE, DAD (BECAUSE JESUS RECONCILED WITH US)

The second stage of the process involved seeking reconciliation, the act of restoring a broken relationship. We've forgiven the offender, now the challenge is to rebuild the relationship with him. In short, peace, Dad. Recall that while forgiveness is always possible, reconciliation is sometimes impossible because it takes two to reconcile. While we reviewed several factors in being able to reconcile, the prime teaching here is that reconciliation is not a one-time event but rather a process that may take years, be erratic, and test the patience of both people. Through Jesus' teaching of reconciliation in His Sermon on the Mount (Matthew 5:23-26), the prime lesson is that reconciliation with both friends and enemies is what God commands. Follow my example, as I follow the example of Christ...by reconciling, if possible, with your dad.

CHAPTER 8   THANK YOU, DAD (BECAUSE JESUS ENCOURAGES THANKFULNESS)

In the third stage of the process, now that we've forgiven our father and are working towards reconciliation, the natural next step is to thank him. We gave a straightforward definition of thankfulness as a feeling or expression of gratitude. As with reconciliation, we reviewed some of the reasons why we turn aside from thankfulness, but, again, none of them are justified. Through Jesus healing ten men who have a skin disease (Luke 17:11-19) we learn from Him the main lesson here regarding thankfulness: Jesus prizes thankfulness for God and what He is doing. It was here that I challenged you, if possible, to contact your dad in whatever method you feel most comfortable with (written letter, phone call, text, meet for breakfast, etc.) and thank him. Or, if this isn't possible, write a thank you letter to your dad and share it with your family. Again, if you feel comfortable, encourage other dads by sharing your letter either publicly or anonymously with us at http://www.AFaithfulDad. org/thankyouletter.

PART 3 HOW DO I CARRY IT OUT?

CHAPTER 9 LIVE FOR GOD

We've laid the necessary groundwork for both restoring and building relationships, so now it's time to get down to the tactical methods of carrying it out. Living for God is the heart of this guide, something I and many of us struggle to do. Jesus' teaching in Mark 12:28-30, a review of the Shema of Deuteronomy 6:4-9, highlights that loving God is the most important all the commandments. Further, Jesus makes the critical connection in John 14:15 (NLT), "If you love me, obey my commandments." And again soon after Jesus expands in John 14:23 (NIV), "Anyone who loves me will obey my teaching. My Father will love them, and we will come to them and make our home with them." So, loving God and living for God are intimately tied together. To sum up, LOVE God and LIVE for God with all you've got – now *that's* a lasting legacy! Here I encouraged you, among other ways, to worship Him, pray to Him, evangelize to others, spend time with Him, trust Him, and listen to Him. Living for God: Our common sense tells us there's really no other way to live. Our common experience, on the other hand, shows us that this is no easy task. Yet, it's the most exhilarating way of life you could ever imagine. Go there with God, and lead your family in the Way.

CHAPTER 10 LIVE FOR OTHERS

As we've demonstrated, living for God is not only the most important of the 613 commands of Mosaic Law, but it's the centerpiece of leaving a lasting legacy. And, since each of us is created in God's image (Genesis 1:27), it's pretty easy to see how living for others holds the position of the second most important commandment. There are no commandments greater than loving God and loving your neighbor, which I'll broadly designate as loving others. Just as we love God in the way we live, we also demonstrate our love for others in the way we live – as self-centric or others-centric. This included all political affiliations, nationalities, different religious beliefs, family, friends, and others. I encouraged you to carry out your love for others by adjusting your thinking, praying for and with others, spending time with others, engaging in hospitality, listening to others, deferring to others, celebrating with others, and, of course, forgiving, reconciling with, and thanking others. Remember: Live out your faith and build your legacy by living for others.

CHAPTER 11 JESUS DEMONSTRATES HIS OWN LASTING LEGACY

Jesus demonstrates His lasting legacy through one of the Bible's most vulnerable stories: Jesus washes His disciples' feet (John 13:1-17). Recall that just prior to Him celebrating the Passover meal in the Upper Room, Jesus' disciples had incredulously argued in contradiction of Jesus' teaching which of them was the greatest (Luke 9:46) and whether the apostles James and John could have the honor (over the other disciples) of sitting at Jesus' left and right hand (Matthew 28:20-28). Undeterred and grace-filled as always, Jesus taught them a gentle lesson in a demonstration of sacrificial service by taking on the role of a menial servant who washed His disciples' feet. But the **prime lesson**, the overarching theme of Jesus washing His disciples' feet, is how Jesus so tangibly demonstrated His own supreme commitment to <u>living for God</u>, who ordered Him to the cross, and to <u>living for others</u>, by dying for us on the cross! Jesus provided the ultimate legacy of service: washing their feet was simply a prelude to history's grandest, humblest act of servitude: taking on the sin of man for our redemption. Jesus knew the vast majority of us would never be crucified or even martyred, so He gave His disciples and, in turn, us, a simple example of how to leave a lasting legacy – His legacy – by sacrificial service.

CHAPTER 12 LEGACY CARRIED OUT IN MY LIFE'S MOST VULNERABLE MOMENT

Lastly, by God's grace, I had the privilege of serving my own dying dad, Gary "Smoke" Zimmerman in his final days. Despite my shameful reluctance to serve Dad in this way, Jesus modeled the behavior and the Holy Spirit guided me to obey the Father's command to serve Him by serving others. I left a final challenge for you to consider what vulnerable act of service God is calling you to perform. Knowing this, I further challenged you to now serve outside of your comfort zone.

CHAPTER 13 QUESTIONS:

1. In your own words, how would you explain a lasting legacy?
2. As a faithful dad, why is it so critical that we follow the Faithful Father?
3. What are some of the joys and challenges you've experienced living for God and others?

14

CONCLUSION

I BEGAN *A FAITHFUL Dad's Guide to Legacy* with a simple premise: What legacy do you want to leave for your family? And God revealed through the Apostle Paul's teaching that our legacy was never really about us in the first place: it's about Jesus!

Follow my example, as I follow the example of Christ.1 Corinthians 11:1 (NIV)

Though it's been five years since Dad's passing, God used the preparation and writing of this book to serve not only as an example of His faithfulness to my family and others, but also for an opportunity to appreciate, grieve, and celebrate my own faithful dad's life, Gary "Smoke" Zimmerman. My prayer is that, in taking on A Faithful Dad's Legacy Challenge, you endeavor to build your own family legacy as you lead your family by following Christ.

Humbly and lovingly we can each joyously proclaim, "I'm a faithful dad, because I follow *The* Faithful Dad!"

CHAPTER 14 QUESTIONS:

1. How has God used A Faithful Dad's Legacy Challenge to grow you closer to Him and your family?
2. Are you ready to make the claim, "I'm a faithful dad"?
3. Who else needs this guide? Share a copy of this guide with three buddies.

THE END

End of Chapters 1 – 14
Individual/Group Questions

Chapter 1 Questions:

1. What's one tradition your family passed along to you?
2. A legacy – a lasting legacy – is about you, Dad, wholeheartedly following Jesus and leading your family to do the same. Why is this true?
3. Consider **CHALLENGE #1**: In what ways have you tried to build a legacy that seemed worthwhile, but ultimately could not stand the test of time?

Chapter 2 Questions:

1. When times turn tough do you find that you drop to your knees and pray?
2. **The Reality:** Whether you know it or not, you're already leaving a legacy now. But what legacy?
3. Consider **CHALLENGE #2**: Honestly answer the big question, "What legacy do I want to leave for my family?" Now, share your answer with your family.

CHAPTER 3 QUESTIONS:

1. What parallels do you see between Paul leading his churches and you leading your family?
2. So how do I strike the right balance between modeling my own example and modeling Christ?
3. Consider **CHALLENGE #3**: How will you and your family commit to memory 1 Corinthians 11:1?

CHAPTER 4 QUESTIONS:

1. Travis claims that being a dad is God's highest privilege to men, because being a dad encompasses so much of what God has created us to be. How so?
2. How can we claim to be a faithful dad?
3. Consider **CHALLENGE #4**: How will you and your family praise God, our Faithful Father, for the opportunity to model your own fatherhood after His perfect example?

CHAPTER 5 QUESTIONS:

1. Did your dad have any "Man Rules" and, if so, what were they?
2. Why is it so important to remember that we have a heavenly Father who NEVER makes mistakes, who ALWAYS loves us, who NEVER forsakes us?
3. Consider **CHALLENGE #5**: Based on your situation, how will you be able to meet this challenge?

CHAPTER 6 QUESTIONS:

1. Why is it usually easier to hang onto unforgiveness than to simply forgive?
2. How would you sum up Jesus' The Parable of the Unmerciful Servant (Matthew 18:21-35)?
3. Consider **CHALLENGE #6**: Based on your situation, how will you be able to meet this challenge?

CHAPTER 7 QUESTIONS:

1. Why can reconciliation be so difficult?
2. What are some similarities and differences between forgiveness and reconciliation?
3. Consider **CHALLENGE #7**: Based on your situation, how will you be able to meet this challenge?

CHAPTER 8 QUESTIONS:

1. Why do we sometimes turn aside from thanking others?
2. How would you sum up Jesus the time when heals ten men who have a skin disease (Luke 17:11-19)?
3. Consider **CHALLENGE #8**: How will you accomplish this challenge?

CHAPTER 9 QUESTIONS:

1. Do you know any "dead men walking" and could you be one of them?
2. In living for God, what's at least one practical way you can carry it out?
3. Consider **CHALLENGE #9**: What change(s) do you need to make to better live for God?

CHAPTER 10 QUESTIONS:

1. So, who are the "OTHERS" God calls us to love?
2. In living for God, what's at least one practical way you can carry it out?
3. Consider **CHALLENGE #10**: What change(s) do you need to make to better live for others, especially your family?

CHAPTER 11 QUESTIONS:

1. Why was Jesus washing His disciples' feet so shocking to the Apostle Peter?
2. What would you say is a main lesson of Jesus Washes His Disciples' Feet (John 13:1-17)?
3. Consider **CHALLENGE #11**: How does Jesus' supreme example of living for God and others impact your view of your own lasting legacy?

CHAPTER 12 QUESTIONS:

1. Why is it sometimes so difficult for us to understand what God has called us to do?
2. When it comes to serving in hard times, how do you interpret the saying, "don't lean away from it, lean *into* it?"
3. Consider **CHALLENGE #12**: What vulnerable act of service is God call you to perform? Now, serve outside of your comfort zone.

CHAPTER 13 QUESTIONS:

1. In your own words, how would you explain a lasting legacy?
2. As a faithful dad, why is it so critical that we follow the Faithful Father?
3. What are some of the joys and challenges you've experienced living for God and others?

CHAPTER 14 QUESTIONS:

1. How has God used A Faithful Dad's Legacy Challenge to grow you closer to Him and your family?
2. Are you ready to make the claim, "I'm a faithful dad"?
3. Who else needs this guide? Share a copy of this guide with three buddies.

Notes

Chapter 1
Charles River Editors, *American Legends: The Life of Billy Graham* (North Charleston, CreateSpace, 2015), i.

"Legacy," Merriam-Webster, accessed March 28, 2016, http://www.merriam-webster.com/dictionary/legacy.

"13 Bizarre Stipulations in Wills," Mental Floss, accessed March 28, 2016, http://mentalfloss.com/article/22633/13-bizarre-stipulations-wills.

Chapter 2
Jim Croce, "Bad, Bad Leroy Brown," released March 20, 1973, ABC Records.

Chapter 3
Eric Liddell, *The Disciplines of the Christian Life* (Nashville, Abingdon Press, 1985).

Henry H. Halley, *Halley's Bible Handbook with the New International Version, Deluxe Edition* (Grand Rapids, Zondervan, 2007), 16.

Chapter 4
Housefires, "Good Good Father," released September 9, 2014, Housefires.

"Faith," Merriam-Webster, accessed March 28, 2016, http://www.merriam-webster.com/dictionary/faith.

"What are the different names of God and what do they mean?" accessed March 28, 2016, http://www.gotquestions.org/names-of-God.html.

"How many times in Scripture God is referred to as Father in the New Testament?" accessed March 28, 2016, http://www.answers.com/Q/How_many_times_in_scripture_God_is_referred_as_Father_in_the_New_testament.

"What does it mean that God is our Abba Father?" accessed March 28, 2016, http://www.gotquestions.org/Abba-Father.html.

CHAPTER 5
Harry Chapin, "Cat's in the Cradle," released October 1, 1974, Harry and Sandra Chapin.

"Finished a day teaching, 'a day wasted,'" accessed March 28, 2016, https://historytech.wordpress.com/2010/04/12/finished-a-day-of-teaching-a-day-wasted/.

U2, "Sometimes You Can't Make It on Your Own," released February 7, 2005, U2.

Everclear, "Father of Mine," released September 25, 1997, Art Alexakis.

Casting Crowns, "American Dream," released October 7, 2003, Mark Hall.

Johnny Cast, "A Boy Named Sue," recorded February 24, 1969 (released July 26, 1969), Shel Silverstein.

CHAPTER 7
Philip Yancey, interview by Lillian Kwon, Christian Post Reporter, on October 2, 2010 at http://www.christianpost.com/news/interview-philip-yancey-on-us-christianity-faith-that-matters-47031/.

The Electric Ben Franklin accessed on March 28, 2016, http://www.ushistory.org/franklin/quotable/singlehtml.htm.

CHAPTER 8

Mark Twain quotes accessed on March 28, 2016 at http://www.goodreads.com/quotes/78468-when-i-was-a-boy-of-14-my-father-was.

CHAPTER 9

St. Augustine, Great Sinner Turned Great Saint accessed on March 28, 2016 at http://www.traditionalcatholicpriest.com/2014/08/28/st-augustine-great-sinner-turn-great-saint/.

The Sixth Sense, directed by M. Night Shyamalan, featuring Bruce Willis and Haley Joel Osment (Buena Vista Pictures, 1999).

Frank Sinatra, "New York, New York," released June 21, 1977, Fred Ebb and John Kander.

"What is the human soul?" accessed March 28, 2016, http://www.gotquestions.org/human-soul.html.

"Iraqi Christians are targets of cleansing, committee told," accessed March 28, 2016, http://www.canada.com/ottawacitizen/news/story.html?id=e7649576-0ebe-4b4f-b803-9a2c64449c41.

"U.S. Leadership Ushers New Age of Christian Martyrdom," accessed March 28, 2016, http://www.frontpagemag.com/fpm/260431/us-leadership-ushers-new-age-christian-martyrdom-raymond-ibrahim.

Ralph Waldo Emerson quotes accessed on March 28, 2016, http://www.goodreads.com/quotes/11079-what-you-do-speaks-so-loudly-that-i-cannot-hear.

CHAPTER 10

John Wesley quotes accessed on March 28, 2016, http://www.goodreads.com/quotes/12757-do-all-the-good-you-can-by-all-the-means.

"Others," Pastor Jack Hyles, accessed on March 28, 2016, http://www.jesus-is-savior.com/Books,%20Tracts%20&%20Preaching/Printed%20Sermons/Dr%20Jack%20Hyles/others.htm.

"Dietrich Bonhoeffer," accessed on March 28, 2016, https://en.wikipedia.org/wiki/Dietrich_Bonhoeffer.

"Nelson Mandela," accessed on March 28, 2016, https://en.wikipedia.org/wiki/Nelson_Mandela.

"Todd Beamer," accessed on March 28, 2016, https://en.wikipedia.org/wiki/Todd_Beamer.

Plato quotes accessed on March 28, 2016, http://www.goodreads.com/author/quotes/879.Plato.

Ernest Hemingway quotes accessed March 28, 2016, http://www.goodreads.com/quotes/353013-i-like-to-listen-i-have-learned-a-great-deal.

Frank Sinatra, "My Way," recorded December 30, 1968, Paul Anka.

Kool & the Gang, "Celebration," released 1980, Ronald Nathan Bell, Claydes Charles Smith, et. al.

CHAPTER 11

Andrew Dumas quotes accessed on March 28, 2016, http://www.inspirationalstories.com/quotes/alexandre-dumas-the-merit-of-all-things-lies-in-their/.

Gary M. Burge, "John," in *Baker's Commentary on the Bible based on the NIV*, edited by Walter A. Elwell, 867. Grand Rapids, Baker Books, 1989.

Chapter 12

Frontotemporal Dementia accessed on March 28, 2016, http://memory.ucsf. edu/ftd/.

Chapter 13

Wade Boggs quotes accessed on March 28, 2016, http://www.brainyquote. com/quotes/quotes/w/wadeboggs311617.html.

"Legacy," Merriam-Webster, accessed March 28, 2016, http://www.merriam-webster.com/dictionary/legacy.

INDEX OF SCRIPTURE REFERENCES

BSB   *Berean Study Bible*
Glassport, PA: Berean Bible (2016)

CEV   *Contemporary English Version*
New York, NY: American Bible Society (1995)

ESV   *English Standard Version*
Wheaton, IL: Good News Publishers (2011)

GWT   *God's Word Translation*
Grand Rapids, MI: World Publishing, Inc. (1995)

HCSB   *Holman Christian Study Bible*
Nashville, TN: Holman Bible Publishers (2009)

ISV   International Standard Version
Bellflower, CA: ISV Foundation (1996)

NASB   *New American Standard Bible*
Anaheim, CA: Foundation Press (1973)

NET   NET Bible
Garland, TX (1994)

NIRV *New International Reader's Version*
Colorado Springs, CO: Biblica (2014)

NIV *New International Version*
Colorado Springs, CO: Biblica (1978, 1984, 2011)

NLT *New Living Translation*
Wheaton, IL: Tyndale House Publishers (1996)

TLB *The Living Bible*
Wheaton, IL: Tyndale House Publishers (1979)

CHAPTER 1

1. Isaiah 40:8 (NLT)

CHAPTER 2

1. 1 Kings 11:6 (GWT)

CHAPTER 3

1. Matthew 17:5 (NIV)
2. 1 Corinthians 11:1 (NIV)
3. Ephesians 3:8-9 (non-version specific)
4. 1 Corinthians 15:9 (NIV)
5. Philippians 3:5-6 (TLB)
6. Acts 9:4 (ESV)

7. Galatians 1:23-24 (BSB)
8. Acts 20:24 (non-version specific)
9. Colossians 1:15-18 (NLT)
10. John 15:13 (ISV)
11. Acts 2:36 (ISV)
12. Genesis 18:22-33 (non-version specific)
13. 2 Corinthians 12:7-9 (NIV)

CHAPTER 4

1. Mark 14:36 (BSB)
2. Hebrews 11:1 (NIV)
3. Psalm 18:25-26 (GWT)
4. Hebrews 11:6 (NASB)
5. 2 Corinthians 5:7 (NET Bible)
6. Matthew 17:20 (GWT)
7. 1 Samuel 13:14 (non-version specific)
8. Matthew 5:3-12 (NIV)
9. Exodus 34:6 (NET Bible)
10. Lamentations 3:22-23 (NIV)
11. 1 Corinthians 10:13 (NIV)
12. 2 Timothy 2:13 (ESV)
13. Matthew 6:11 (non-version specific)
14. Psalm 91:4 (NIV)
15. Psalm 68:5 (ESV)
16. Ephesians 4:6 (NASB)
17. Matthew 4:19 (non-version specific)
18. Genesis 2:24 (non-version specific)
19. Deuteronomy 6:4-9 (non-version specific)
20. 1 Corinthians 3:10-15 (non-version specific)

21. Proverbs 27:17 (non-version specific)
22. Ecclesiastes 3:1 (non-version specific)
23. Exodus 20:12 (non-version 20:12)

CHAPTER 5

1. Hebrews 4:16 (BSB)
2. 1 Corinthians 11:1 (NIV)
3. Hebrews 13:8 (ESV)
4. 1 Corinthians 11:1 (NIV)
5. Joshua 1:5 (non-version specific)
6. 2 Corinthians 12:9 (non-version specific)

CHAPTER 6

1. Matthew 6:14-15 (NIV)
2. 1 Corinthians 11:1 (NIV)
3. Matthew 18:21-35 (NIV)
4. Luke 23:34 (NLT)
5. Acts 7:60 (ESV)

CHAPTER 7

1. Colossians 1:19-20 (NIV)
2. Mark 11:25 (non-version specific)
3. Colossians 3:15 (non-version specific)
4. Matthew 7:16 (BLB)
5. John 3:16 (non-version specific)
6. Matthew 5:23-26 (NIV)
7. Matthew 9:13 (BSB)

CHAPTER 8

1. John 11:41-42 (CEV)
2. Luke 17:11-19 (NIRV)

CHAPTER 9

1. Philippians 1:21 (ESV)
2. 1 Corinthians 1:18 (NIV)
3. Mark 12:28-30 (NIV)
4. Deuteronomy 6:4-9 (non-version specific)
5. John 14:15 (NLT)
6. John 14:23 (NIV)
7. Matthew 10:2 (non-version specific)
8. Mark 3:16 (non-version specific)
9. Luke 6:13 (non-version specific)
10. Acts 1:13 (non-version specific)
11. Acts 4:13 (non-version specific)
12. Acts 6:7- 7:60 (non-version specific)
13. 2 Corinthians 11:23-29 (non-version specific)
14. Exodus 23:25 (NIV)
15. Genesis 1:27 (non-version specific)
16. 1 Thessalonians 5:17 (non-version specific)
17. Matthew 28:18-19 (non-version specific)
18. 1 Peter 2:12 (non-version specific)
19. Psalm 42:1-2 (non-version specific)
20. Psalm 57 (non-version specific)
21. Proverbs 3:5-6 (non-version specific)
22. Matthew 14:22-33 (non-version specific)
23. Romans 8:28 (non-version specific)
24. Luke 9:35 (non-version specific)

CHAPTER 10

1. John 13:34-35 (NIV)
2. Genesis 1:27 (non-version specific)
3. Mark 12:28-31 (NIV)
4. Luke 6:32-36 (HCSB)
5. Philippians 2:3 (non-version specific)
6. 1 Timothy 2:1 (non-version specific)
7. 1 Thessalonians 5:11 (non-version specific)
8. Hebrews 13:2 (ESV)
9. Proverbs 19:20 (non-version specific)
10. Proverbs 2:2 (NLT)
11. Luke 14:11 (non-version specific)
12. Proverbs 11:2 (non-version specific)
13. Luke 14:7-14 (non-version specific)
14. Mark 9:37 (BSB)

CHAPTER 11

1. John 13:17 (NIV)
2. Luke 22:12 (non-version specific)
3. Matthew 26:29 (non-version specific)
4. Luke 9:46 (NLT)
5. Matthew 20:20-28 (ISV)
6. Matthew 28:24 (ISV)
7. John 13:4-5 (non-version specific)
8. John 13:1-17 (NIV)

CHAPTER 12

1. Isaiah 61:3 (NIV)
2. John 13:12-17 (NIV)
3. 2 Corinthians 12:9 (NIV)
4. 1 Corinthians 11:1 (NIV)

CHAPTER 13

1. 1 Corinthians 11:1 (NIV)
2. 2 Corinthians 12:9 (NIV)
3. Matthew 18:21-35 (non-version specific)
4. Matthew 5:23-26 (non-version specific)
5. Luke 17:11-19 (non-version specific)
6. John 14:15 (NLT)
7. John 14:23 (NIV)
8. Genesis 1:27
9. John 13:1-17 (NIV)
10. Matthew 28:20-28 (non-version specific)

CHAPTER 14

1. 1 Corinthians 11:1 (NIV)

Made in the USA
Middletown, DE
23 September 2016